GR
STRAWBERRY

GREEN STRAWBERRY

Gerard Melia

HODDER AND STOUGHTON
LONDON SYDNEY AUCKLAND TORONTO

Copyright © 1988 Gerard Melia

First published 1988

British Cataloguing in Publication Data
Melia, Gerard
 Green strawberry.
 1. English language. Readers
 I. Title
 428.6'2

ISBN 0-340-42360-9

All rights reserved. No part of this publication may be reproduced or
transmitted in any form or by any means, electronically or mechanically,
including photocopying, recording or any information storage or
retrieval system, without either the prior permission in writing from the
publisher or under licence from the Copyright Licensing Agency
Limited. Details of such licences (for reprographic reproduction) may be
obtained from the Copyright Licensing Agency Limited, of 33–34 Alfred
Place, London WC1E 7DP.

Typeset in Monotype Lasercomp Bembo by Cotswold Typesetting,
Gloucester.
Printed in Great Britain for Hodder and Stoughton Educational, a
division of Hodder and Stoughton Ltd, Mill Road, Dunton Green,
Sevenoaks, Kent by Richard Clay Ltd, Bungay, Suffolk.

Contents

	Note to the Teacher	vi
1	JUST ANOTHER DAY	1
2	A LADY CALLS	17
3	INTERLUDE IN PARIS	32
4	TRAPPED IN THE DOCKS	45
5	THE END FOR LEROY	63
6	A TIGHT SPOT	71
7	DAD HELPS OUT	80
8	THE SECRET OF THE WARDROBE	88
9	A PRISONER	98
10	IN THE NET	112
11	THE PICK UP	121
12	AFTERMATH	133

Note to the Teacher

This is the story of a boy living in the Docklands who is a diabetic. Two years ago I attended a clinic for diabetics. Whilst there, I became fascinated by the way young diabetics came to terms with their body chemistry. It was heartening to see the will and determination that they brought to bear upon themselves as they continued to lead normal lives.

This novel also reflects my daily experience of Docklands and the ambition of some of the resident adventurous spirits to better themselves.

As with all books in this series, suggestions for classroom use and discussion can be found in the accompanying support material.

Gerard Melia
February 1988

1

Just Another Day

The alarm on the bedside clock buzzed. The alarm under the pillow clanged. Slowly stretching out an arm, Alan pressed the button on the bedside alarm. Reaching beneath the pillow he took out the round, red alarm clock, switched it off and placed it face down on the lino.

He sat up, stretched, yawned loudly and scratched the back of his head. It didn't itch. He'd scratched his head ever since he could remember.

'Are you up, Alan?' a voice screeched from the bedroom across the corridor. 'Alan! Alan, I'm talking to you . . . are you up?'

'Yes, Mum.' His throat was parched and dry. A cold had forced him to breathe through his mouth for the last couple of nights. His throat was as sharp as a razor when he swallowed. Colds had to be watched, the nurse had said.

Standing by the bed he stretched once more. He stretched so much he became a little dizzy. He felt he was about to fall.

'Alan . . . are you sure you're up?'

'Yes, Mum . . . I'm up.'

'Alan's ability to sleep through an earthquake was legendary. He'd been a very quiet baby. Oversleeping, however, was something he really couldn't afford to do.

He flicked the bedroom curtain aside. The window was hazed with condensation. A pool of water dripped from the edge of the windowsill onto the lino. He bent down and picked up a handful of damp tissues which he'd used

in the night and thrown onto the floor. He used the drier parts to wipe the mist from the window pane. The tissues absorbed the water, becoming a multicoloured pulp in his fingers. He threw it into a cardboard soap powder box he used as a waste paper basket.

Squinting through the window, he checked the familiar landscape of Canning Town. Yes . . . there it was, just like yesterday. From the seventeenth floor he could see the white concrete flyover. Early morning traffic was already queuing to get over into Commercial Road and down into the Blackwall Tunnel and beyond. In the distant left of the picture, St Paul's ballooned creamy white amidst the square skyscrapers of the City of London. In the tower block opposite a woman was hanging out her daily quota of nappies with one hand, and holding her baby in her other arm. The nappies billowed and waved in the breeze which swerved between the blocks of flats. One hundred and twenty feet below, the litter flicked and flirted with the yellowing grass and dusty shrubs. As Alan glanced beyond the other tower blocks, he could see the disused cranes and the long sheds throwing black shadows across the empty, sunlit docks. A jet liner scored the blue sky with two broad chalk lines.

'A Jumbo 747 . . . British Airways . . . for Heathrow,' Alan muttered. 'One of these days I'll be sitting on one of them . . . getting out of here.'

Alan didn't like this part of London. They'd had a nice three-bedroomed house in Plaistow, three miles away near the station until his Dad had had those wonderful schemes for making money. His mother, Marcia, had sold the house and applied for a council flat on the Springfield Estate. The name was a puzzle. The area had never ever been a field. Louise, in researching a project for her GCSE history exam, discovered it had all been marshland and used for fattening sheep; but that had been in the time of Henry VIII. Building the Royal Docks there had not improved the area. During the war it had all been flattened in the blitz. There was a park, mostly populated by stray dogs, a football pitch with an artificial surface, an open-air swimming pool that was always closed for repairs, seven derelict cars and twelve pubs. No way could it ever be described as a 'residential area with amenities' – there weren't any!

Marcia Hogan hated the place. She'd gone up to the council offices and complained loudly and banged the counter till she was forcibly removed by two clerks and the doorkeeper.

'Springfield Estate!' she bawled out. 'What's bloody springy about it? It's dirty, noisy, rundown, in need of a can of paint and graffitied with obscenities. It's a bloody dump. Would you live there?' She poked a vicious finger into the Housing Officer's chest. 'It all ought to be blown up and forgotten, that's what you ought to do. We'd be better off in cardboard boxes under Blackfriars Bridge!'

The men were kind but insistent. As they pushed her through the door she shouted up the Town Hall stairs in the general direction of the Mayor's Parlour.

'Why we vote for you lot I'll never know! We'd be better off plaiting sawdust!'

Even the doorkeeper remembered that and mentioned it to the Chairman of the Housing Committee, but nothing happened. The council was short of houses for everybody. There were thousands on the waiting lists. Some people had been waiting for two years. You just had to get by as best you could.

Alan shuffled into the small, narrow bathroom. He filled the basin with hot water and washed his left thigh. Reaching into the cupboard he pulled out a plastic box. Taking out a cotton wool swab he dipped it into a bottle of methylated spirit and rubbed it onto his thigh. He fitted a needle into a syringe and inserted it into a small bottle containing a colourless fluid. Holding the syringe upwards, he gently pressed the plunger till the fluid spurted from the end of the needle. Selecting a place at the top of his thigh, he inserted it. There was just a minute pricking sensation. Depressing the plunger slowly, he administered his insulin injection. Alan was a diabetic. Every morning at 7.30 he had to administer two injections. The first one would answer his body's immediate need for dealing with breakfast. The second injection of insulin was mixed with a zinc solution so that the insulin would be released slowly throughout the day. He'd got used to the rotten business now. Two years ago in the junior school they'd found him in a coma lying on the toilet floor. That's when it all came out. The doctor at the hospital asked him all the usual questions like 'Have you felt thirsty a lot recently?' Alan told them he'd felt thirsty for months. He admitted stealing money from the teacher's handbag to buy cans of orange juice. He just had to drink something. He got into trouble through going to the toilet a lot during lessons and having drinks of water all the time. It all came out, but the doctor said it wasn't his fault. His Dad went mad and blamed it on his mother for working overtime at the canteen in Tower Hamlets. Dad always blamed her every time anything went wrong. He blamed her if a light bulb went or if the telly broke down. He even blamed her when it rained in Rhyl when they went to Wales for a week's holiday in Uncle Arthur's caravan. Trust her to pick the wrong week, he said. When he found out about Alan's diabetes he said it must be on her side of the family. None of his relations had ever had diabetes and he made out as if it was Marcia's fault.

His mother never said much. She wasn't a talkative person. Louise reckoned that Dad had married Mum because she left so much space in the conversation for Dad to fill.

'That's probably what he found attractive in her in the first place,' Louise confided. 'You see, when people are going out together they always show their best side . . . like when I go out with Danny I always show him the best side of my character . . .'

'Danny Platting must be in difficulties then!'

'What?'

'Danny . . . he hasn't got a good side at all . . . he's a plonker . . . a big, soft plonker.'

Louise didn't go red and grab his hair like she usually did. She paused and gazed out of the window, apparently searching for inspiration from the view of the Barking Road and the Jewish Cemetery.

'Well . . . that's what going out with men is all about . . . finding out if they are . . . plonkers . . . or not.'

Alan washed himself. He checked in his Dad's shaving mirror to see if the hairs on his chain warranted a shave. At thirteen years of age he was very anxious to use the shaving soap that bloomed white and creamy from an aerosol can. Rubbing his chin he experienced little stubble resistance on his finger tips. He could leave the razor alone till the weekend when he had more time to indulge himself in the mirror. He loved looking in the mirror. The reverse convex side enlarged every pore in his skin. The hairs up his nose were black and shiny, the blue in his eyes was really blue and green and bits of yellow, and when he screwed his eyes up he could make the black hole in the middle alter its size. Alan found his features a constant source of fascination. He often wondered, as he gazed directly at himself, where the person of Alan Hogan really was. He assumed the real Alan was situated fixedly behind his wide, blue green eyes.

He washed out the syringe and threw the needle into the waste bin. Whatever he imagined himself to be, there was no escaping the fact of his diabetes. For the rest of his life he would have to live an orderly and exacting life style in which what he ate or drank would be measured and calculated to prevent him having a hypo – a kind of fainting sensation – when the sugar levels in his body dropped below normal.

It had been difficult. He hated needles and injections. They'd been very good at the clinic in Barking. The nurse had shown him how to do it and he'd practised on an orange for a few weeks. He'd never forget his first injection. He cried for twenty minutes.

Alan heard Louise getting up. Well, to be more accurate he heard her stereo suddenly blast out before she plugged her headphones in. She was into heavy rock and everybody for four floors down knew about it. The old lady above – Mrs Cartwright – was stone deaf so it didn't bother her. She often said how delighted she was to be on the top floor – nearest to God and the birds, so she said. Albert, the caretaker, was very good to her when the lift broke. He always saw to her groceries and milk. She never went short – everybody saw to that. Mrs Cartwright had done her share for the people round the flats. She'd delivered meals on wheels for seven years, up and down the lifts, till her knees went. She could hardly bend them now.

Alan went into the kitchen, put the kettle on, placed three eggs in a pan of water on the stove, and shoved two rounds of white sliced bread into the toaster. He set out three basins on the breakfast bar and filled two with cornflakes and one with bran. His mother was very conscious of her health now that she was just forty years of age. She had a theory that fibre would sort out all her insides. Everything she ate contained a high fibre content. Alan got the impression that she was packing herself out like flock in a pillow so that there was no room for surplus fat and no space for upsetting bugs to breed in. She had started to eat lots of oranges, lemons and grapefruits to keep colds and 'flu at bay after reading an article in a shopping magazine about vitamin C. She was mad about Satsumas and bought them in pounds when they were available, but she still got colds just like everybody else. She insisted, talking through a blocked nose, that her colds didn't last as long as theirs. Alan never took note of how long his colds lasted, he was just glad to get rid of them. It didn't strike him as a matter for open competition.

He buttered the toast, scooped the eggs from the boiling water with a dessert spoon and got a bottle of milk from the fridge.

Louise came into the kitchen, clasping her dressing gown around her middle. She'd lost the belt when she'd gone on a field trip to Gloucester with the Fifth form. Now she usually used one of Dad's old ties but she'd lost that too. She was very careless with clothing. She once took a coat and skirt to the cleaners and forgot all about them. When she remembered two months later they'd been sold.

She sat down and poured milk on her cornflakes. Louise never spoke to anyone before ten o'clock because of her moods.

'Nobody, not no one, must speak to me till I've got myself going, not unless they want a thick ear. By lunch time I've got myself sorted out. Before that, walk on eggs, our Alan . . . do you hear?'

Alan had learnt over the years to leave her alone. He quite welcomed these quiet, moody moments together.

'I reckon we are much closer together like, when we say nothing. It's when we start to talk that we fall out,' he confided to his mother one day.

Marcia had smiled knowingly. She'd felt the same about her husband, Fred. He often talked himself dry and frequently forgot what he'd started talking about in the first place. Fred had plenty of chat but it never amounted to anything. It was like firing a shot gun – plenty of noise and bits and pieces of talk flying off in different directions. He always had a scheme . . .

'This is the big one,' he would begin. Marcia would raise her eyebrows and reach for her *Woman's Realm*. His schemes were imaginative and preposterous. Once he decided to breed ferrets because he thought he could export them to Australia to keep down the rabbit population. Another time he bought a consignment of two thousand mirrors that would make fifty pence a mirror – £1,000 – which he'd put on a dog at Walthamstow at 7 to 1 and make £7,000 and they'd all go to Bermuda for the sun. He broke half the mirrors unloading them from the van into Mrs Cartwright's garage at the bottom of the flats. On yet another occasion he was conned by a Greek chef in Leyton into investing in a new substitute for fresh cream in cakes. The chef was prosecuted for the misuse of dangerous chemicals. Marcia had threatened him with the police if he took any part in another swindle in which two of his mates sold Christmas cards for a fictitious charity. 'Make a bomb,' he said.

Alan missed him. He was always attracted by his Dad's eager-eyed optimism. Things were going to turn out right and there was always another scheme, 'the big one, Alan . . . the real big one, son.'

One day, two detectives turned up at the flat to interview Fred about a robbery. Somebody had nicked a lorry-load of whisky from a bonded warehouse in the Victoria Docks. Alan could tell from his mother's face that she knew something about it. Alan remembered with a sudden twist of his gut Dad's 'big win' two weeks previously at the dog track. He'd come home and thrown ten pound notes all over the settee.

Dad's alibi turned out to be Biddy Sullivan from Balance Street. She went to the County Court and swore he'd spent the night with her. It was reported in the local press. Marcia didn't go out for a week. The day Dad walked a free man from the Court, Marcia banned him from the house. They divorced a year later.

Alan missed his Dad despite his criminal record. He seemed to offer excitement, a bit of colour, a possible escape from a life of aching dullness.

Louise slowly and deliberately knifed a dollop of marmalade onto her toast. She smoothed it out across the buttered surface so that every small section of the toasted slice was evenly covered. It was a slow, methodical process. It reminded Alan vaguely of a TV Do-It-Yourself programme on brick laying.

'Tea or coffee?' he asked. It was the only question he was allowed most mornings.

'I'll have tea this morning,' she replied through a mouth of sticky crumbs. She ate loudly. Her mouth, partly opened, permitted Alan a glimpse of the toast and marmalade being moved around and masticated, like the inside of a cement mixer. The squelching and swallowing could put you off food for the whole day. He envied her ability to eat marmalade. He'd tried the special diabetic marmalade from the chemist but it had affected his bowels in a memorable way. It had been very embarrassing at school but Mr McDonald, the Headmaster, had been understanding because his wife had diabetes too.

'What are we going to do then?' The toast crunched like a nut between crackers.

The question took Alan by surprise. Was he supposed to answer or was it a rhetorical question? Was she just thinking aloud? He decided to wait and see. He said nothing.

'Well?' she said in a demanding tone.

'Well what?' Alan replied. He didn't want to overdo things at this time of the morning.

'Are you stupid? Sorry, silly question . . . I know you're stupid. Let me spell it out for you.' She leaned forward and using a remaining finger of toast spelt out the sentence. 'What . . . are . . . we . . . going . . . to do . . . about . . . our holiday . . . at . . . Maldon . . . with our Dad? Got it? Pin head!'

'I haven't given it a lot of thought. I wasn't sure it was on.'

'Why? What's to stop us going?' she muttered, layering best butter on another slice. She liked to let the toast cool off so that the butter lay thick and unmelted on the surface. She hated soggy toast. 'It's the only holiday we're likely to get.'

'Are you sure Mum would want us to go?'

'Why not? We've been before.'

'Yes . . . but now he's got another girlfriend . . .'

'That's his business.'

'Yeh . . . but Mum would get very upset!'

'Leave all that to me. You just get a paper job for spending money and I'll do the rest.' She looked at the final sliver of toast before ramming it into her crumby mouth.

Louise stood up, grabbed her plate and cup and placed them in the sink. Turning on the hot water she spurted a dash of washing-up fluid on the plate and watched the water turn it into a froth of bubbles.

'What time did she come in last night?' she asked.

'About one o'clock . . . I think. I was only half awake. Mum did a double again.' Alan placed his plate and cup in the sink.

'That's three double turns in a fortnight. What's got into her?'

'Well, she did say that she'd take us on a holiday abroad . . . perhaps she's determined we won't go to Maldon.'

'That's really stupid. There's lots of things to sort out – Dad's debt on the furniture for a start – before we consider expensive holidays.'

Alan remembered his anger when he'd first cottoned on to the business of the furniture. It had been bad enough Dad leaving – and he had had to leave after what happened – but to leave them in debt for the furniture, the telly, the washing machine . . . well, that was a real cheek. When Alan realised that Dad had taken the radio and cassette recorder, and they weren't paid for either, he really blew up. When he shouted down the telephone, his Dad hung up, but Alan went on shouting as though Fred was still listening. It was all so unfair. Fred had gone off to fend for himself and left Mum to sort out the wreckage.

Mum, as usual, absorbed the worst of all the problems the divorce provoked. She was the soft, giving, understanding side of the arrangement. Even now when the maintenance payments didn't arrive for weeks, sometimes months, she just got on with things.

It was because of her common sense and forgiving nature that the children went for a few weeks to Maldon every summer. She wasn't happy that Alan and Louise should be cut off completely from their father. He wasn't a regular visitor; he never took advantage of the court order allowing him a weekly visit. He was always 'away on business' or 'too tired' or 'had a touch of bad luck. I don't have the fare' – that kind of thing. Lying came quite easily to him. It was a special skill he had. Alan once saw him coming out of a new Greek restaurant in Forest Gate with two women, and watched him get into a new Sierra GT and drive off towards Romford. That was just after he'd 'phoned Mrs Cartwright upstairs to ask her to tell Alan and Louise that he was broke at the moment and he'd send their Christmas presents when he was 'better fixed'. There were good times of course. At Maldon he'd got himself a little dinghy and the three of them would go out fishing. Alan didn't catch much but the whole out fishing. Alan didn't catch much but the whole business of getting bait and casting the lines and waiting was great fun. The dinghy was called 'Loallan' after the pair of them.

Alan pulled on his jacket and began preparing his school lunch. He always had wholemeal bread with cheese and pickle, an apple and two digestive biscuits to be eaten with a mid-morning cup of tea which was provided specially in the school office by Miss Pritchard, the school secretary. The nurse at the clinic called it 'Compulsory Biscuit Time'. Like everything else to do with his diabetes it was now a routine and he didn't think much about it.

He packed his games bag with two textbooks, an exercise book containing his unfinished homework essay, his trainers and his shorts. He checked his inside pocket for his tube of glucose tablets. If for some reason his body extracted too little sugar from his food he would have 'a hypo'. He'd feel a vague panic, a sudden hunger and sweating, and his pulse would race along. Occasionally he'd get 'rubber legs' and have difficulty walking in a straight line. Anyone not in the know would assume he'd been drinking. One glucose tablet under the tongue usually did the trick and he was as right as rain in ten or fifteen minutes. Taking out his wallet he checked his identity card which stated that he was a diabetic and winked at the photograph he always carried of his hero Gary Mabbat, the England and Spurs footballer. He was diabetic too. Alan got ragged a lot at school about supporting Spurs because all his mates supported West Ham.

'I'll leave it to you then, Louise. It's OK by me if we go to Maldon.'

He opened the kitchen door and walked down the

passage to the front door. A letter snapped through the letter box. Picking it up he read the address, turned round and came back into the kitchen.

'It's a letter for you, Louise . . . looks important . . . could be a job. See you.'

Louise looked at the outside of the envelope. She'd seen quite a few recently. In a month's time she was to take six GCSEs and she'd been looking for a job. She didn't like school and hadn't worked much throughout her five years at Westmoreland Road Comprehensive. When Dad left home she had a bad patch and truanted for a month. She was caught working in a hairdressers in Barking when the Deputy Headteacher, Miss Radcliffe, called in to make an appointment to have a perm; Louise had given Shirley, the manageress, a false name and address. In Miss Radcliffe's room a day later Louise was asked why she'd played truant. She wasn't very talkative at first but Miss

Radcliffe was an old campaigner; she had seen and heard it all before.

'Is it because your father has left home?' she asked.

'Partly, Miss . . . but . . .'

'But what?' insisted Miss Radcliffe.

'Well, it seems to me that as I grow older, most people make some allowances for the fact. But school, well, as far as school is concerned, I'm just a fifth year pupil. I'm a first year that's grown too big for school uniform. And as for what we get taught, I'm not really into the amoeba, or book-keeping or the Thirty Years War.' She paused, wondering whether to continue with her outburst. She decided to risk all. 'Anyway, Miss Radcliffe, I'm glad you found me out in that hairdressers. I was getting bored out of my tiny mind. It solved the problem of how to get out of it.'

Louise felt better after saying that. She preferred the truth – most of the time. Now that she was running the house whilst her mother was at work, she felt mature and a little more confident, ready to risk talking about herself.

Louise opened the letter. It was from a local printing firm.

'Dear Miss Hogan,' it said. 'Having received a favourable report from your school we are anxious to arrange an interview. A vacancy has arisen in our Accounts Department. Your headteacher expects you to pass in six GCSEs, including Mathematics and English which we would accept as adequate qualifications for this post. Please ring Miss Prescott on ext. 778 as soon as possible. Yours faithfully, Meredith Jones.

Taking the letter to the sink she ripped it into pieces and threw it in the trash can.

'I don't want a job in Accounts, thank you! I don't want a job in a hairdressers or Sainsbury's or British

Home Stores. I want a different kind of job, an interesting job, that's what I want.' She often talked to herself when she was alone in the flat. Gazing through the window she could see Alan walking across the bridge over the motorway. 'I'm responsible for him, the poor sod. In the end it's going to be just me and him. There's nobody else going to help us. Mum and Fred have had it. It's all down hill for them. Well, they're not bloody well taking us with 'em!'

She dried the dishes, folded the cloth and placed it on the radiator. Taking the salt and pepper pots she opened the cupboard and placed them on the second shelf. On the top shelf she saw a plastic cylinder with her Mum's name typed on it. 'Mrs Marcia Hogan, take three times a day.' It was her Valium tablets.

'No . . . I'm sorry, Mum. We're going to do it our way.' Louise banged the cupboard shut. The sound echoed through the thin walls of the flats and disturbed her mother but she soon turned over and fell back into a deep sleep.

2

A Lady Calls

Alan strolled down Dunstan Street, passed the Dick Archer Primary School and up onto the footbridge which crossed the dual carriageway. He always stopped and watched the traffic. Huge lorries and trailers from the Continent passed beneath him. Lorries from Spain, Hungary, France, Belgium and Holland. They'd come over on the ferries to Dover or Folkestone, cross the river at the Dartford Tunnel, and made their way to London. Added to this stream of heavy vehicles was the traffic from Tilbury Docks, and the commuters from all parts of Essex as far as Southend. All of them bustling and shouldering their way into the City of London to begin the day's work. It made this stretch of road one of the busiest in Europe.

Glancing at his watch Alan calculated he still had time to do a detour down Albert Road so that he passed Andertons Garage. On the forecourt in front of the display window they had a collection of BMWs for sale. They were all secondhand but still very expensive.

On each visit to the forecourt he would tour round the vehicles, checking on their mileage, noting the engine capacity and admiring the upholstery and fittings. When he started work, he'd decided he was going to buy a BMW. Cars and driving were his passion. His Dad had had a car before the trouble – a Ford Cortina 2 litre – which had taken them on holidays and for days out. Alan had steered and changed gear whilst it was in a car park, with his Dad controlling the foot brake. When he came out of hospital Alan asked the doctor whether he'd be allowed to drive. To his delight he was assured that diabetics, whilst not allowed to drive a bus or pilot an airliner, could drive a private car.

When his father went away he left the car for Marcia and the kids. It had to be parked on the street because they had no garage. One night it was jacked up and all its wheels removed. The car radio was ripped out and the vandals attempted to start a fire on the back seat. The corporation workmen removed it. Marcia now had a bike for getting to work and they all used public transport. The effect of this was to increase Alan's yearning for a BMW. Some nights when he found sleep difficult he would imagine himself climbing into a BMW Coupe, wearing the white overalls and helmet of the rally driver. His arms and legs would be covered in coloured patches advertising soap, cigarettes, diesel oil, spare parts and cocktail drinks. At the green light he would let in the clutch and dive into an immediate lead, grinning into his side mirror at the looks of astonishment on the faces of Nigel Mansell and Nelson Piquet.

'You may be the best Grand Prix drivers,' he would shout to them, 'but when it comes to rally driving, Alan Hogan is Mr Big. Hogan is No. 1.'

After several circuits of Brands Hatch, in which he lapped all the other cars, he would fall into a deep and satisfying sleep. A smile would settle on his relaxed countenance; perhaps he was enjoying the victory wreath around his neck or spraying his fans with a large bottle of champagne.

Gary, the garage salesman, knew Alan well. He shared Alan's enthusiasm for fast cars and privately enjoyed watching Alan examine and stroke each car as though he were a judge at a cattle show.

As Alan caressed the highly polished bonnet of a 2 litre job in grey and black, Gary came out onto the forecourt carrying a mug of tea and a thick bacon sandwich.

'How now, my son.' (He always called Alan his son.) 'Come into money have we? Now, let's see . . . 2 litre, sunroof, stereo, white walled tyres, one owner from new, 37,000 on the clock, well . . . let's see . . . $5\frac{1}{2}$, no . . . 5 to you . . . 5 thousand readies . . . OK? Now, is it cash or credit card, my son?

He laughed and launched his mouth deep into the bacon sandwich. A piece of rind got stuck in his teeth. In trying to remove it with a podgy, nail-bitten finger he caused a cascade of greasy crumbs to tumble down his navy blue double breated suit. The suit was new. The Directors of Andertons Garage were keen to move further up market into high status cars. It was important the salesmen looked polished and efficient. Gary was struggling to achieve the same sleekness as the cars. The diet he'd tried for a month had not fulfilled his expectations and the bacon sandwich was about to add to the perceptible bulge supported by his double breasted jacket.

'Of course I could make you a . . . very . . . special offer, my son. And don't take it too naughty . . . 'cos it's well meant. How about putting in a good word for me with your Mum . . . eh? Nothing but the best, you understand, for a lady of that class . . . a good night out . . . in a BMW, of course . . . up West? We was friendly years ago . . . she knows me. How about it?'

This suggestion did not take Alan completely by surprise. Louise had raged to him some weeks ago about the way Gary always ran down the forecourt when Mum went past on her way to the shopping precinct.

'He's guilty of sexual harassment!' she shouted. 'He

ought to be reported.' But she wasn't sure who to report it to.

Marcia hardly seemed to bother. She just half smiled and then after a few polite words like 'How's your mother keeping, Gary?' and 'Where's your Judith working now?' she'd sidetrack his obvious intents into family matters. She'd known him and his family for over twenty years. He didn't pose any threat to her.

Alan's first inclination was to thump Gary in the soft middle of his new suit. There were two good reasons why he didn't. Gary would cancel the lucrative arrangement he had with Alan for cleaning the BMWs on Friday nights and Saturday mornings. The second reason was that Gary was very handy with his fists himself and could cause serious damage to a person's general health.

Since his father's departure, Alan had become very protective towards his mother. He assumed that his mother would now stay single and that he would, in the course of time, take his father's place and look after her in her old age. The idea of another man muscling into his mother's circle of affection was not welcome. Looking at Gary as he stuffed the greasy remains of the bacon into his mouth, he felt, quite frankly, that Gary wasn't good enough. His father didn't rate very highly in Alan's estimation, but Gary was a definite non-starter in the list of potential substitutes. He'd heard Louise and his mother laughing about their ideal man – the looks of Cary Grant and plenty of money. Gary wasn't in that class.

'You'd get a ride, now, in these cars . . . you know . . . delivery to customers . . . or collecting 'em from our Knightsbridge showroom. You'd have to wear your best suit, of course. Tell you what, tell her I'll take her to Paris. She knows it well . . . eh?'

This proposition brought together in Alan's mind two

competing notions. One was the rejection, without further consideration, of Gary's date with his mother and the other was the attractive and persistent dream of ownership of a BMW. Alan's fertile imagination had scurried quickly beyond the mere idea of travelling in a BMW from Knightsbridge. Alan wasn't wearing his best suit. He was clothed in the white overalls of the rally driver. He'd been spotted by the Director of Andertons Garage, Mr Spottiswood, and was now sponsored by them. Blazoned on his helmet, as he placed it over his head like a medieval knight he'd seen in *The Adventures of Robin Hood*, were the words 'Alan Hogan, Andertons Garage, London'.

It doesn't take long for such a train of thought to pass through the mind, but the hesitation it caused before Alan replied gave Gary the hope that Alan would swallow the bait and ask his mother.

'Does she like musicals?' Gary asked, keeping up the pressure.

'What?' Alan was still climbing into a BMW at Brands Hatch.

'Does she like things like . . . *Evita* . . . *South Pacific*, that kind of show?'

'I don't know. I don't remember her going to the theatre much.'

'There you are then . . . new experience for her.'

'It's not up to me. Why don't you ask her yourself?' He was trying to shift the responsibility back on to Gary's shoulders. Gary detected a weakness.

'Now look, sunshine. It's not that I haven't asked her. I've asked her out dozens of times.' Lying came easily to Gary, it was part of his job. 'It's just that I think she feels that you and your sister might take offence . . . so she doesn't bother. Now, if you get my drift, if you was to

mention it and sort of indicate you thought it was a goer of an idea, well, she could change her mind.'

Alan couldn't see a way out of this except to say,

'Well . . . Garry. I've got to get to school now. I'll think about it.'

'Just you think about it, my son. Oh, and whilst you're here. A mate of mine, Tommy Glover, he's a Security Guard at Gate 3 Victoria Docks. He reckons the police pulled a body out the dock last Thursday night. Now I know that you and your mate Leroy muck about in the Sheds at the Victoria. I've seen you climbing over the fence. Just you watch it, sunshine. There's lots of things happen down there it's best not to know about.' Gary tapped the side of his nose with a thick greasy finger. 'I'm doing you a favour, son. Your Mum has enough on her plate without you getting into bother, OK?'

'How was he . . .?'

'Strangled with a piece of wire . . . then drowned . . . so my mate reckons. Very nasty. Smuggling they say. Lots of it about. So don't you forget. Put a word in for me with your Mum and I'll see you get a few rides up West. OK, sunshine?'

Westmoreland Comprehensive School was only two streets away. It had been built ten years before the Second World War and it was a single storey building constructed in the form of a square. The inside quadrangle had a covered walk all the way around it, a twentieth century attempt to copy the cloisters in a medieval monastery. Like most of the property in the area, it had been bombed in the London blitz and one side of the square had been removed. Into it had been inserted a double storey building housing the science laboratories and a new staffroom. Added to its left corner was a new games hall whose doors opened out into the only green patch in the area. This 'playing field', as it was called by everybody, was surrounded on all sides by the housing of a council estate.

The foyer of the games hall was a busy spot first thing in the morning. The shop run by the Parents Committee was opened at 8 o'clock by Nelly Armstrong, a retired school cleaner. She sold lunch packs made of fresh bread rolls filled with ham, cheese, egg, salad or jam. Blackcurrant jam rolls were very popular. Crisps, sweets, chocolate and soft drinks were also on sale.

Alan always met Leroy here. It was a challenging situation for a diabetic. Everything available for sale would break his dietary control system. Occasionally, if he forgot his morning biscuits, he could buy a packet from Nelly, but the habit shared by many of his classmates of regular purchases of crisps, soft drinks and chocolate was forbidden. It would simply make him very ill. Leroy Harris, however, had no such inhibitions. Each morning he met Alan there and regularly consumed three packets of cheese and onion crisps, a can of orange juice and then slipped two packets of biscuits into his satchel in case he felt a pang later.

The two had become friends through the one thing they had in common – a health problem. Leroy was an asthmatic. The brotherhood of those who have spent time in hospital was a strong bond and they'd become friendly when they'd spent periods together in the school library instead of taking part in PE lessons.

Leroy had bad patches when he needed his respirator to help his breathing. Alan wondered on some occasions if Leroy would ever recover from these wheezing attacks, but he always did. They both loved sport. Leroy got into the lower school basket ball team without too much trouble with his asthma, but there were periods when he just sat in the library and tried to read. It was because of this that he'd developed a surprising interest in the plays of Shakespeare. It was a source of considerable amusement to the rest of the class who found Mr Wilson's literature lessons on *Macbeth* a real bore. One of Leroy's homework essays entitled 'The problem of ambition in *Macbeth*' was read out by Mr Wilson and praised. Leroy was very embarrassed. He didn't hand in the next essay but after a private chat with Mr Wilson, who promised never to read out any more of his essays, he handed in his work normally. The teacher contented himself with writing supportive and encouraging comments at the end of each piece. Leroy also discovered that without making a big effort he could remember whole speeches by heart. This fascinated Alan who couldn't remember his home 'phone number. He'd sit opposite Leroy in the library with the

Shakespeare text open in front of him whilst Leroy, with little prompting would reel off the scenes, changing his voice for different characters. It was a talent and skill he never shared with Mr Wilson . . . just in case.

They had one other thing in common. Leroy's father lived in Jamaica. He'd been brought up by his mother and his five sisters. He hadn't seen his Dad for four years.

Alan waited whilst Leroy bought his crisps. They went down the lower school cloister and sat in their form room. It was 8.45 and form time began at 9 o'clock when Miss Twist came and called the register and gave out the notices for the day.

'This fellah at the garage . . . well, he's interested in my Mum.'

Alan felt he could trust Leroy.

'What about it?' asked Leroy, licking his fingers to get at the last crumbs of cheese and onion.

'Well, it's not right, is it?'

'Depends,' muttered Leroy.

'What do you mean?'

'Depends whether your mother fancies him.'

'I'm sure she doesn't.'

'Well, there ain't no problem then.' Leroy seemed to be losing interest in the conversation.

'But he's asked me to ask her whether she'd go out with him.'

Leroy looked at him and smiled.

'If he can't ask himself . . . it's no game for him, man.'

'I suppose you're right . . . yes . . . but . . .'

The sentence that was to follow was never said. The lure of a ride in a BMW with all its possibilities disappeared. Alan knew in his heart it wasn't much of a bargain and with somebody like Gary you never knew if he'd keep his promise anyway.

'No,' he muttered to himself as Miss Twist called the register. 'I'm not going to do it. If he can't ask himself, that's it.'

During the morning break he went to the school office and had his tea and biscuits. It was raining. He went along the cloister and sat down on the wooden bench next to Leroy and watched the rain.

'We had trouble with a lodger once.' Alan had noticed on previous occasions how Leroy's conversation could be random and surprising.

'Yeh. When my Dad went back we took in a lodger . . . a real snappy dresser . . . on the dole but he earned ready cash in the snooker club in Manor Park. Cash, nobody ever knew how much, but he paid regular. Well, after a while he got a bit familiar with my sister Bernice and he chatted up my Mum too. When he came home one night all his clobber was out in the garden. He made an awful fuss and threatened to do her in but Ellery Johnson, him that spars at Tunny's Gym, came round and told my Mum not to worry. He'd see to him. And he did. We ain't seen sight nor sign of him since.'

'Is he still around . . . this Ellery Johnson?'

'He lives with us now. He married Bernice.'

'So if my Mum got into a fix, I could ask Ellery to . . .'

'Why not? He's heard about you from me. He knows we're mates. He's very obliging . . . in that way.'

Alan felt a little of the responsibility of mother-caring lifting from his shoulders. He'd often wondered what he'd do if some really rough trade attacked them in the night. Well, now he had a possible solution – a quick phone call from Miss Cartwright upstairs to Leroy, and Ellery Johnson would come along and do the necessary.

'Would he help us out if we got into trouble in our Shed?'

Leroy chuckled. 'Trouble in Shed 31? It's deserted, derelict. There's never anybody there on our side of the dock. That's why we picked it, remember?'

'Gary, at the garage, says the police dragged a body out of the dock on Thursday night.'

'Who was it? Did he say?'

'No, he didn't.'

'Take no notice of him. He's just trying to scare you.'

'Do you think so? I'm not so sure. He says it's a favourite place for villains. 'Course he could be pulling my leg, I suppose.'

'If they'd got a body out, it would have been in the papers.' Leroy ripped open another packet of cheese and onion crisps.

'The police might want to keep it out of the press.'

'Stop worrying, Alan. We can look after ourselves.'

'Oh yes.' Alan sniggered. 'We're the ideal pair for the heavy stuff. I'm a diabetic and you can't breathe properly on a bad day. We'd certainly scare the living daylights out of the Krays!'

Even Leroy had to laugh at that.

'Well, if it helps, Alan, I'll have a word with me mother's minder, Ellery. He has contacts. He'd know. I'll see what he says. All right?'

Alan nodded but he was still uncertain.

'There's a lady wants to see you, Hogan.' Miss Twist was passing on her way from the staffroom. 'She's out in the staff car park causing quite a stir. Half the staff are out there, seeing if she needs any help. You'd better get down there before the bell goes otherwise all our male teachers will be late for lessons.' Miss Twist bustled off. She was not in a good mood for her next class, whoever they might be.

'I'll come with you,' said Leroy. He'd discovered the

attraction of girls last year when he fell in love with the girl cashier at the Savoy Cinema. He saw the same film five times one week, just to talk to her at the desk.

'Come on, Alan. We better be quick or we'll have to go to maths.' They both hated maths. It was algebra this morning and they hadn't done the homework. They'd been set the problem of calculating how long it took to fill a bath of water with two taps.

'I can't see the point of this,' Alan had grumbled. 'When I have a bath I put the taps on and read a comic. When it gets over my chest I turn the taps off. Now why do I need algebra for that?'

When they got to the car park they soon spotted the staff chatting up the lady in the car. Alan walked towards them. Mr Wapping, the lower school PE teacher, saw him.

'Here he is . . . young Alan Hogan . . . here's the man of the moment. Hurry, Hogan! Can't keep the lady waiting!'

As the group moved away, Alan saw the car. It was a D registration BMW Cabriolet, 2 litre.

'God God,' he thought. 'That was quick. Perhaps Gary was so keen . . .' Then he saw the driver. He recognised her from the photograph Louise had shown him before she threw it in the bin. Sitting behind the wheel, tapping her fingers on the dashboard in time to the stereo was Connie Masters . . . Dad's new girlfriend.

She was smartly dressed in a primrose wool jumper, a white silk blouse bubbling up around her neck. Her blond punk styled hair was pulled to one side by a tortoiseshell comb. Her make-up was brushed and shaded to emphasize her high cheekbones and her lips were outlined in black.

Seated in the rear of the car, reading a newspaper, was a large, bulky man, wearing a seaman's cap and a chunky

navy blue sweater. His thick grey hair fell in greasy curls onto his shoulders and dandruff flecked the headrest on the rear seat. The man ignored Alan.

'Hallo, Alan.' Connie extended her hand. Three fingers were ringed. The middle one supported an expensive looking diamond. 'Pleased to meet you. I'm Connie. Your Dad asked me to call, knowing I was in the area. We'd like to know when you and Louise are coming to Maldon, if you're coming at all, that is?'

There was a tone to her remarks which indicated that she wouldn't be too disappointed if they didn't go.

'Yes . . . yes . . . we'll be coming. We were talking about it this morning . . . first two weeks in August . . . like last year . . . if that's all right?' Alan caressed the bright sheen of the car door. 'Is this yours?'

'Yes. Got it last week . . . bit of luck at Walthamstow dog track . . . your Dad made a bit as well. That's partly why we want some idea of when you're coming so that we . . . your Dad and me . . . can arrange our own holiday. OK?'

She started the engine. It purred like a contented cat. Letting the clutch out, she slowly drove away.

'Tell Louise to drop us a card confirming the weeks in August and some idea of the time of your arrival at the bus station and I'll pick you up. OK?'

'Yes. Yes, fine,' stammered Alan. He couldn't take his eyes from the car. Connie glanced left and right at the school gate and filtered smoothly into the traffic. The man in the seaman's cap threw his paper crossly onto the front seat beside Connie.

'Hey! Oh yes! Hey, Leroy! We'll be driving around in a BMW on our holidays. How about that? Wait till I tell Mum.' Alan paused. No. He wouldn't tell Mum. She'd get upset at things like this. Alan was growing up. He was becoming sensitive to the situation. Not putting his foot into things all the time.

'Didn't like the look of the dude in the back seat. He doesn't want you to go to Maldon, I can tell you that for sure. He looked like trouble to me. Who is he?'

'No idea,' Alan replied. He'd concentrated all his attention on Connie.

'She's a smart piece. Who is she?' Leroy was very impressed.

'Oh she's . . . a friend . . . a friend of the family,' Alan said. Leroy gave him a quizzical look.

'You don't have to be shy with me, man. I know all about these things. It happens all the time to lots of people. You'll get used to it . . . you're not Hamlet.'

'Hamlet?'

'Yeh . . . he came back from college to find his father

dead and his mother married to his uncle. He was pretty screwed up about it.

"A little month, or ere those shoes were old
With which she followed my poor father's body,
Like Niobe, all tears – why she – even she –
O God! a beast that wants discourse of reason
Would have mourned longer – married with my uncle ..."

He was really tight up about it, man.'

'I don't think Mum will marry again . . . and not Gary . . . that's for certain.'

'Nothing's for certain, Alan.' Leroy pointed to the school gate. 'Your Dad's done all right for himself.'

Alan decided there and then to talk to his mother about things.

3

Interlude in Paris

Marcia Hogan rode her bike home as usual. As she passed Andertons Garage, Gary waved to her. She waved back.

'He's a fool,' she thought to herself, 'but harmless.'

She remembered when she was at dancing school with his sister Judith. He was the grubby, snotty little fellah they rescued from the big ditch at the back of Wildsens Chemical Works. He'd been on the make, as usual, running with betting slips to the bookie's office in Belstow Road. Each lunch hour he'd skip out of school and make his way to the back of the works canteen which overlooked the railway line and 'the pong river' as it was called. The men would pass the betting slips through the canteen window and at 4 o'clock he would return with the winnings . . . now and again! They tipped him a few bob and the bookie, Arthur Mills, was generous to him around Christmas time. He was ten years of age. It was all illegal, of course. That's why he fell in the stinking brook. Constable Winick was visiting the gateman when he saw Gary 'acting suspiciously'. In the chase Gary fell head first into the brook. PC Winnick couldn't find him. He was puzzled by such a quick disappearance and he gave up. The gatekeeper, Peter Wood, told his mother and she sent Judith and Marcia to fetch him. He had to be stripped when he got home and all his clothes were burnt in the back yard. The smell was appalling and they couldn't get the black tar out of his hair so he was shaved, bald. Now here he was, Mr Smooth, selling secondhand cars.

'It's amazing how people turn out,' she mused. Here's

this scraggy little lad, never much of a beauty, now in a position of some responsibility. There was little Bertie too . . . Bertie Tring. Well, he was nothing at school . . . could hardly read . . . now he owned the biggest furniture removal business this side of London. A big house in Romford and a dolly bird wife. You couldn't tell . . . school isn't a good predictor of how you are going to get on in life and there was Fred . . . well, he'd been a catch . . . or so she thought . . . but that was another story.

Louise and Alan had prepared the vegetables as usual. It was stew tonight and she'd bought the stewing steak on her way home. With the help of the pressure cooker they were sitting down helping themselves from the bowl of stew in an hour.

Mealtimes were quite special for all three of them. In some strange way they felt the need to talk and discuss anything and everything. Dad had started it. He'd read in a book somewhere that the family that talks together stays together. After he'd gone, the habit persisted. In fact, there seemed to be a greater need to communicate between themselves in order to compensate for the crevasse which had opened in their family relationships. It was now an established behaviour and as a mark of its high status the television was never switched on at mealtimes.

'There's an advert for a special offer in the paper, Mum.'

'Oh?' Marcia was busy chasing a carrot in the stewpot.

'Yes,' persisted Louise. 'It was an American trench coat . . . looked great.'

'Well it would, wouldn't it? That's what adverts are for . . . to make things look great.'

'That's right,' Alan said grinning. 'Who ever heard of an advert not making something look good.' He put on

an American accent. 'Roll up, folks. Only a few left . . .
dud batteries. I can guarantee that these batteries wouldn't
light a glow-worm . . . totally useless . . . but to you . . . a
favoured customer . . . £27 each . . . a bargain.'

'Oh, shut up and talk sense,' rasped Louise. She was all
right when she was handing out the aggravation but she
was a poor receiver. 'They were American Women's
Army Corps coats . . . they were top quality.'

'Did you notice anything about the advert . . . the
picture for instance?' Marcia asked.

'Well . . . no.' Louise was puzzled by the question.

'When the illustration is hand drawn, not a photograph,
watch out! They can make a drawing look like anything.
Photographs, like those in a Spencers catalogue, are more
detailed . . . more reliable. Things are not what they seem
when it's a drawing. I never send for anything that's
advertised as a sketch.'

'Photographs aren't that reliable either,' piped up Alan.
'That holiday photograph of Louise taken at Margate . . .
she looked quite glamorous. Well, I mean . . . just look at
her in real life. Who'd buy her?'

Louise went red and grabbing the ladle from the stew
attempted to break the knuckles of his right hand as it
rested on the table. She missed. Marcia grabbed her arm
quickly and took away the weapon.

'Come on now, you two. Alan, just behave yourself!
More stew?'

'I'll kill him . . . I will . . . I'll kill him!' Louise was
upset. She was between boyfriends at the moment. She'd
just been dropped by Alvin Bradshaw for an older girl
who worked in the chemist's in Albert Road. Her Dad
was worth a few bob and had bought her a Mini City for
her birthday. Alvin dropped Louise after his first ride.

'A bird with wheels,' Alvin said, 'has distinct social

possibilities.' This could only mean he'd be expecting her to give him a lift to the night matches at West Ham United. Girls, food and football . . . that was it for Alvin. Nothing else ever crossed his mind. To have her waiting for him in the car after the match and to be taken to a sit-down chippy was it! What more could a fellah want? Well . . . perhaps plenty of vinegar and a big bottle of tomato sauce.

'Only pulling your leg, sis,' Alan said regretfully. He didn't like upsetting her.

'Things are never what they seem. No, they certainly aren't,' mused Marcia as she poured herself a second cup of tea. 'Your Dad was considered a bit of a catch . . . I was thought a bit of a trollop . . . appearances aren't very reliable.'

'Why did people think you were . . ?' Alan asked.

'A trollop? Well, in them days people's attitudes to young girls was different . . . we had to behave ourselves or else.'

'Or else what?' Louise persisted.

'It goes back to the time I was a dancer. You wouldn't think when you look at me that I was a dancer, would you? Judith and me . . . that's Gary's sister . . . we was the stars of The Miss Brigman Academy of Dance. Dolly Briggs was her proper name, Brigman was her professional tag. She had the lease on two small warehouses at the back of Solly Bernstein's sweat-shop, just off Katherine Road. One was leased to Solly as a stock room and the other she had done up as The Dance Academy. She'd been a ballet dancer somewhere in Germany before the war, so she said. She knew what she was about when it came to the dance exams. Me and Judith passed 'em all . . . with honours. She pointed out, however, that we'd never make the big ballet companies because we were too big . . . me at the top,' she indicated her bosom, 'and Judith was developing rather large at the back . . . the lower back.'

'You mean her bum was too big.' Alan liked to get things right.

'Well, yes . . . it was . . . not much call in ballet for those kind of measurements.'

'Yes . . . I've noticed that on the telly . . . these ballet dancers are all on the thin side . . . and you're right, they don't carry much luggage at the back, do they!'

'That'll be all, Alan. Go on, Mum. What happened?' Louise loved Marcia's stories.

'Well, one day Dolly Briggs brings in a cutting from a paper advertising for "Dancers in French Cabaret". Auditions were to be held in Islington.'

'"Ask your Mums," she said, "if it's all right for you to go to auditions." She had this funny fractured way of talking. "I take you up there to theatre . . . I know most of people in this business . . . they're sharp if you not watch them . . . I could pull a string or two . . . and the money can be good after a year or two when your legs mature."' Marcia laughed as she remembered. 'Judith looked at her legs to see if they was maturing when Dolly said it . . . it was as if Judith expected 'em to change colour or something!'

Marcia moved to the edge of the armchair as the memories returned. 'Now, I was fourteen, coming on fifteen in two weeks. You left school at fifteen in them days so I wasn't bothered about that . . . but mother . . . well, that was something else.'

'She was strict with you, wasn't she?' prompted Louise as she felt herself being drawn into the story.

'She brought us up like she'd been brought up herself. My Dad was a Sergeant in the Grenadier Guards, killed in the war in Korea in 1950, so she was extra strict. "I don't want to see you ever do anything what your Dad wouldn't want you to do," she used to say. She thought my Dad was up there watching us all the bleedin' time. She never married, although she had offers. We owned the house we lived in. We was the only people who owned their own house in our street and her sister had done well and married a man in business in Shrewsbury. But she never married. She didn't think Dad would have approved. Sleeping with another man would have been adultery for her.'

'Adultery?' Alan always asked questions calculated to embarrass.

'Behave yourself, Alan,' Louise said impatiently. 'Go on, Mum. What happened . . . did you get the job?'

'Yeh . . . course we did. Judith and me was the best dancers that day . . . and Dolly did pull a string or two. But I daren't let on to my Mum. Over the next weeks I got all my dance kit and stuff to Judith's. She lived in a big rented house with six brothers and sisters, including Gary, and it was a tip . . . you could hide anything there.

'One Friday instead of going to school Dolly took us to Victoria Station where we was met by a chaperone, a Mrs Mather, a nice, plump lady from Liverpool. She took responsibility for our passports and tickets and the like. I'd filled all the forms in myself and forged me mother's signature. She wasn't much good at writing and I did it regular. Dolly, of course, had two letters from our parents giving permission for us to go . . . she was a real old innocent was Dolly . . . we wrote them ourselves too.

'We crossed on the ferry from Folkestone to Calais and from there we got on a train to Paris. God, we were excited. When we came out of the station, Mrs Mather got us a taxi and we drove through the streets of Paris. We couldn't believe it. It was just like on the films. All the road and shop signs were in French and the gendarmerie were just like their photographs . . . the sun was shining and hundreds of people were drinking and talking at tables out on the pavement. You never saw that kind of thing in East Ham or Stratford Broadway. Whole streets would have pavements covered with tables with coloured umbrellas over them . . . and waiters serving drinks. I'll never forget it. It made you smile and feel quite lightheaded . . . as though you would faint at any time. From an ordinary, boring life in East London I was suddenly living on a different plane . . . I was kind of up . . . up somewhere in the excitement of life . . . and Judith kept saying, "Wait till I tell them at Plaistow about this . . . they'll never believe it."'

'"I'll never tell them at Plaistow," I said to myself. "I'll never get the chance . . . me mother will kill me at Victoria."'

'Where did you live?' asked Louise.

'We had lovely digs . . . nothing posh . . . but comfortable. We was looked after by Madame Louise . . . you're called after her, 'cos I never forgot that woman. She was so kind to me. She always had a hot bath running when we got home from the theatre to take the soreness out of our limbs because it was bloody hard work at first. Judith and I weren't used to dancing for an hour three times a day. We were so exhausted some days we slept till ten in the morning. For three weeks I heard nothing from England. I fully expected the French police to pick me up and put me back on the boat. I learnt afterwards that Mum had sent our Billy to fetch me back but they wouldn't let him on the ferry without a passport so they waited until he got one.

'I was just getting the hang of things; I'd got a few words of French, I'd got a little dance to myself in the afternoon show and I was fitting in with the senior girls . . . and the food . . . I loved the food. I was mad about garlic bread . . . and them croissants with jam first thing in the morning with coffee in a cup the size of a bowl. It was fantastic.'

Marcia's face was aglow. Recalling her trip to Paris brought back the very youthfulness she was describing. She was transformed from a drawn, pale, strained woman, to a relaxed, laughing-eyed teenager. She flushed with the memory of it all. It was as though she'd been drinking.

'One night when I got back to my digs, our Billy was sat there. I can see him now, still wearing Uncle Tommy's overcoat, blue trousers, brown shoes and a trilby. I didn't recognise him at first. I never found out where he got the trilby. It gave him a bit of confidence in a foreign country, so he said. He felt like a detective on the trail . . . like in an American film.

'"You've got to come home at once," he said. "You've really upset our Mum . . . and there's to be no argument. The French coppers will be brought in, so start packing."

'Madame Louise shook her head behind him and motioned to me to say nothin' and go upstairs.

'"Will Monsieur be staying the night? I have a small room at the rear of my apartment?" she said.

'"No . . . No, Missis. I'm going as soon as she's packed."

'"Oh, what a pity. We're having such a pleasant spring here in Paris . . . I thought whilst Monsieur was here he would take some little time to look around before he returns to England. It would be a pity, would it not, to come to Paris and not see just a little?"'

Marcia's voice caught the French flavour of Madame Louise's English.

'Her scheme was obvious. She knew I didn't want to go. If Billy could be delayed perhaps he could be persuaded.

'"You mean I could stay here, bed and board for nothing?" Billy was always quick to possibilities.

'"For two nights certainly. After that it's a big cabaret night at the club and my rooms are spoken for, but till then . . ."

'"And no charge?" insisted Billy.

'"There will be no charge, Monsieur."

'Judith who was watching all this was fascinated. "It was like fishing off the pier at Southend," she reported to us afterwards. You could see the bait passing before Billy's mind. First picture was our house in East Ham with our Mum sat there looking stern. Next picture was Billy in a Paris club surrounded by chorus girls. Then another picture of our neighbours nodding their heads as he brought me down the street in disgrace and then another picture of wine, food and him, Billy the lad, living it up and telling the fellahs at the Print Works what a great time he'd had. Madame Louise, whilst all the time keeping prim and proper stance, managed to give the impression that the two days would be quite spectacular and that sin – particularly French sin – would be available.

'"How do I know this isn't some kind of trap to get the money? I've heard how you Frenchies lead people astray just to get the cash . . . you know . . . bobs-your-uncle. You're skinned . . . broke . . ."

'"I will personally guarantee that nothing like that will happen, Monsieur."

'"Sure?"

'"Quite sure, Monsieur."

'Well, that was it. He stayed the two days but Madame Louise was wasting her time. It was all his life was worth to return home without me. It would have been an insult to his manhood.

'I cried the night before we left. Madame Louise cuddled me in her arms. I hadn't felt like a child for years. My mother wasn't a cuddler . . . didn't believe in too much physical contact . . . that was her way. What really upset me was that a few days before our Billy turned up Judith and I had been taken out by Madame Louise and Monsieur Bari . . . he was her kind of boyfriend . . . he'd be about fifty I reckon . . . nice gent. He'd take us to a café on the Champs-Elysées and we'd just sit there and watch the world go by. The war was over now and people were just getting used to the idea of having a good time again. You could hear all kinds of different languages being spoken . . . and lots of rich people in posh cars and flower sellers and a chap playing the piano accordian. He was great. It was real background music to real . . . real life . . . in Paris. I could feel me feet tingle inside my shoes . . . even me stomach was excited. I'd found a place that really gripped me . . . I was part of it now. I had a job, good digs and bit of pocket money. I'd bought me first bottle of French perfume . . . real French perfume. I was throbbing with life. It was a joy to get up in the morning and fling the window and the shutters open. There it was. Paris. There I was. Marcia Smith, a young girl in Paris. It was a beginning . . . and for the first time in my life I felt free . . . that's the feeling I remember most . . . I was free.'

Marcia got up and went to the window of the flat. She swept the curtain aside and looked out.

'He brought me home. On the ferry I said, "Did you like Paris, Billy?"

'"All right I suppose," he shrugged his shoulders. "They don't have proper pubs and the ale is piss." That just about summed it up for him.

'Me mother gave me a good belting when I got home . . . parents believed in corporal punishment in those days. I ended up with two black eyes and a bruised back that I couldn't sleep on for a fortnight. I was "got a job" at Samuel Backs and Co., packing mintoes and aniseed balls in a factory the size of Euston Station, me and 300 other girls, eight till five and Saturday mornings till 12.30. The sweet, sticky atmosphere and the chatter of machines stupefied you. I wasn't allowed back into the Dance Academy because I was a wicked and deceitful girl and not to be trusted. "You'll come to a bad end, my girl, you'll never be any good, you're a trollop." And that was it. Just look out there.' She pointed beyond the window.

Louise got up and stood beside her.

'That's what we've come to . . . opposite, another block

of flats . . . to the left, another block of flats . . . to the right, Silvertown factory, estate and the river. Look at the buzzing life down there.'

As Louise looked there didn't appear to be any movement at all. The streets around the base of the flats were lit with amber lights but they were empty. From the flats, hundreds of lights shone through hundreds of curtains in a rainbow of colours.

'Can you hear the accordian playing? Can you see all these Eastenders enjoying themselves, dancing in the streets, drinking coffee outside the Boulevard Café de Canning Town, and the docks, full of ships from the Orient with foreign sailors bringing a touch of colour to the neighbourhood? And there in the distance the Eiffel Tower . . .'

The docks stretched into the distance, two fretted slabs of water in the moonlight bordered by dark squares of empty sheds, the cranes erect and still like cacti in the desert night.

'They just snapped my life in two . . . the lot of them . . damn their souls . . . the lot of them.' Marcia began to cry. Louise put her arm around her. 'I could have done great things over there . . . my whole life would have been transformed . . . I'd be living in a chateau in France now . . . with a French boy and a French girl . . . and a rich husband with a BMW.' She smiled at Alan through her tears.

'Don't take on, Mum,' Louise said, consoling her. 'You've done well by us . . . hasn't she, Alan?'

Alan came over to the window and between them they manoeuvred Marcia into an armchair.

'Now you just listen to me, you two. Just you make sure that if your chance comes along you take it. Do you hear me? Now you promise . . . any chance to be free of

... of round here.' She waved her hand towards the window. 'Get out as soon as you can ... never mind me ... I'm too late for my gravy train. But you ... get out as soon as you can. If it means exams ... then pass 'em and get the hell out of here. There's nothing for anybody round here ... and the council knows it ... they sent all these no-hopers here, the bad debts ... the fag end of society ... they all live round here ... so first chance you get ... move out ... as far as you can get.'

She pulled out a handkerchief from her sleeve and wept into it.

'Get me one of the tablets, love.'

Louise got up and brought her a glass of water and a Valium tablet. Alan went into the kitchen and started the washing up. Louise came and joined him. They didn't speak. Each was contained by their own thoughts. Mother's Parisian adventure was new to them. They were replaying it in their minds. Neither of them had been abroad. The far-off hills seemed very green. Paris seemed the place for a new life ... a new start ... things seemed much livelier ... everything in the Docklands had suddenly become very grey.

Louise peeped at her mother through the hatch in the wall that separated the kitchen from the lounge. Marcia had put the TV on and turned the sound off. Watching the pictures and mopping her eyes she stretched out her legs ... her dancer's legs. Now they were blue lined and varicosed like a road map of rural Sussex. Thin, tired legs that wouldn't ever dance in Paris again.

4

Trapped in the Docks

Perhaps Marcia's rejection of her surroundings was implanted in Alan from childhood. Now that the Dockland Development Corporation had begun to alter and transform the Old Royal Docks and to find alternative uses for the great warehouses, Alan and Leroy decided to escape the boring ordinariness of high-rise flats by creating a den in which they could savour the change and hope that the Corporation's plans for renewal seemed to promise. Their secret place, a foreman's office in Shed 31, overlooked a flat expanse of water, capable of holding 30 huge cargo vessels. They were fascinated by the great yellow machines that were busy demolishing a line of warehouses to make way for a short-take-off airport (Stolport, it was called in the papers). The cascading brickwork and the clang and creak of collapsing buildings had a particular fascination for them.

They started to furnish their den with pieces from the destruction. One wall sported a metal enamelled sign which read 'P & O Quay 7'. On the opposite wall hung an aerial photograph of the docks and a row of dockers' hooks which they found in a sack.

Marcia's story of her adventure in Paris was buzzing in Alan's mind that Friday night as he and Leroy ducked under the barbed wire, crossed the disused railway line and squeezed themselves between the wooden sleeper fencing that enclosed the Royal Docks.

They knew from their observations that two security guards at No. 2 Gate would be brewing up and that the third guard who normally manned the barrier would be chatting up Maggie Denison, the barmaid at the Hat and Feather just by the dock gate. There was hardly any traffic for the security men to check at this time of night. They seldom raised the barrier more than three or four times during the night shift.

Alan and his friend made their way to the rear of Shed 31. They walked along by the water's edge peering down occasionally to see if anything, or anybody, had been pushed in during the previous night. Since they'd been coming here – about two months now – they'd witnessed some amazing sights from the safety of the private hiding hole.

Two weeks before, Leroy was gazing out across the dock as the rain sleeted down on the cobbled roadway. A car was parked without its lights on. There was a man sitting at the wheel.

'Waiting for a woman do you think?' asked Leroy. They'd become very knowledgeable about illicit affairs. It was amazing the number of couples who used the site for secret meetings.

'Looks like it. Could be something else . . . could be a pick-up . . . something knocked off in town . . . brought out here . . . change cars . . . off to the buyer. It's on *Police Five* every week,' Alan said with the air of someone who saw this kind of thing regularly.

They brewed their tea on a gas ring which somebody had forgotten to disconnect. Holding their mugs in both hands to warm their palms, they watched the car without any great enthusiasm. The sound of a van approaching revived their interest. It stopped about 50 yards behind the car and flashed its lights. A man got out of the van and walked slowly towards the car. He was carrying a heavy bag. The driver of the car got out, went round the back of it and opened the boot. The first man handed over the bag which was placed in the car boot. The driver of the car banged it shut. Then, turning round, he pulled a gun from his pocket and shot the van driver who staggered to his vehicle but collapsed as he attempted to climb back into the driving seat. The lads were petrified. They couldn't believe what they were seeing.

'He's bloody well shot that bloke, the bastard!' Leroy blurted out.

Alan had the presence of mind to place his hand over Leroy's mouth before he shouted something else. The murderer still had the gun. If he knew there were two witnesses they could be next.

Without warning, a battery of lights shone over the whole scene. Dark figures began to move towards the killer. Then the chap who had been 'murdered' got up, dusted his clothes and began talking to the fellow with the gun. The men walking towards them were pushing a camera on wheels. It was a scene from a TV production by the new Whitehouse Productions Ltd who had set up in Docklands to make films for Channel 4.

Alan giggled. Leroy eventually saw the humour in the situation but the mug was still shaking in his clasped hands.

On another occasion, one which was particularly painful to Alan, they watched four cars being driven to the edge of the dock: a BMW; a Mercedes Benz; an Audi Quattro and an old Ford Cortina, a bit of a banger with dents and rust all over it.

The drivers of the three expensive cars got out, released the hand brakes and pushed their vehicles into the dock. Alan stared in wide-eyed astonishment. Then the men got into the old Ford Cortina and drove away.

Alan was so shocked, he told Gary at the garage, in strictest confidence, of course, hoping that the garage would arrange to crane them out and perhaps reward the informant. Three days later the police turned up with two cranes as a result of an anonymous tip off saying that 'hot' cars were being dumped. They discovered 37 cars in the dock, one of which was helpful in a murder enquiry.

The boys' hiding place was at first floor level in Shed 31. An iron stairway led up to the office from the ground floor. The shed itself had been used for receiving and storing heavy cargo from the large merchant ships which had used the dock. It was big enough to accommodate the whole of the Stratford Shopping Centre, huge, dark and empty. The office had a small window which looked out onto the dockside and the three cranes. Everything was peeling. Grey and black paint flakes blew onto the dockside. The cranes looked as though they had developed a tropical skin disease as the flaking paintwork revealed sections of undercoating and rust. A broken door to the crane-driver's cabin waved at them every time the wind blew across the expanse of water. On really windy days they could almost gauge the windspeed by the rate at which the door clanged against the crane's metalwork. Painted in large white letters across the Shed immediately opposite were the initials 'PLA' (Port of London Authority). Lines of liquid rust stripped it as the rain water deluged from the broken guttering. The 'L' was fast losing its bottom segment and in a few months it would disappear completely. Everywhere you looked the view was empty, miserable, useless. The dockscape, once the centre of busy commercial enterprise, was deserted. An industrial cemetery with sheds for gravestones.

The lads, however, had continued to make their little pad as homely as possible. Leroy had found a piece of carpet. It was soiled and threadbare at one end but they put the foreman's chair over that part. There was a sink with running water, the gas ring, and a cupboard in which they kept the tea and sugar dry and the candles in jam jars. In one corner was a metal filing cabinet.

They didn't come every week. Sometimes it would be three weeks before they felt the urge to creep away into this no-man's-land. Friends at school had bragged about the places they had in sheds at the bottom of gardens in Manor Park and one bloke had a fitted-out studio attached to his house where he did his photography and aeromodelling. But their place was extra special because it was secret and illegal. Every visit was a small adventure and they were certain no one else knew about it.

They'd been quite surprised by the bird life. Two herons had nested and brought up their family in Shed 21 across the dock and during the migrating periods a few hundred geese had settled on the water before flying off north. Two of the geese didn't make it; one was caught by a fox and the other by a couple of the wild cats that lived and hunted in the darkness of the sheds.

On this dull, wet evening Alan boiled the kettle and placed three lit candles in jam jars on the table. Leroy took out a book from his pocket and began to read. After washing the cups, Alan dried them with paper towels he'd removed from the dining hall at school.

'What you reading?' Alan asked.

'*Henry IV Part 1*,' Leroy replied.

'Who wrote it?'

'Shakespeare, you twit.'

'Sounds like a history book to me.'

'It's one of Shakespeare's history plays. He wrote a lot of 'em; *Richard III, Henry VI* – three of them – all about the War of the Roses. I haven't read 'em yet . . . but you can get 'em all from the library.'

'I'm not in the library much . . . not much time for reading . . . not with homework as well. After what Mum said last night about leaving the estate, I suppose I'll have to get down to it.'

'Leaving?' Leroy put the book on the table. 'Leaving London?'

'I suppose so. My mother reckons Paris is the place to be. It's very exciting, so she says.'

'I didn't know that French was one of your options? I thought you chose woodwork?'

'I'll have to reconsider my position. You see, apparently Paris is much more enjoyable and exciting than Piccadilly Circus and all that.'

'What will you do? How will you make a living? You don't speak French.'

'It'll have to be show business. My mother was an

international dancer.' Alan tapped his legs to indicate that the talent had been transferred to his own two limbs.

'But you don't do drama at school either. You said it wasn't for anybody who played football.'

'It's in the blood. If your mother or father is in show business . . . well, it's very difficult to avoid it really.' Alan gazed into the flickering candlelight. 'When my mother was telling us last night about running away to Paris I knew that's what I had to do. It's just there inside me.' He pointed to his chest. Leroy looked at his chest. It didn't appear to be particularly special. It looked exactly like the chest Alan had been sporting the day before.

'Can you dance then?'

'I don't know yet. I expect it's there. Well, to be honest I know it is. I have this feeling for it.' Alan was now deep into a dream of his future. Strolling down the Champs-Elysées wearing black trousers, a cloak and a large peaked cap in black and white check, and smoking a long, thin cigar.

'Now, let's get this straight, Alan.' Leroy was smiling. 'You can't speak French, you don't know whether you can dance, your school GCSEs will be in woodwork, maths and geography and you've never been on a stage before in your life . . . but . . . you're going to become a dancer in Paris?'

'That's what I've got in mind . . . yes!' Alan looked a bit defensive. He felt that Leroy was taking advantage of his current state of unreadiness to take the mickey out of him. 'I know you think I can't . . . but . . . well, I only got the idea last night and I'm not fourteen till next November so I've got time to sort myself out. I can change to French in September for a start.'

'But you were hopeless at French!'

'I didn't like Madam Jones . . . her French was Welsh.'

'She manages all right with everybody else . . . she gets good results with the sixth form.' Leroy went back to his book. The whole thing sounded stupid to him. Alan gazed through the window into the blackness of the dock. In the sky above Woolwich he noticed two lights flickering. They seemed to be tied together.

'How many other lads want to become dancers in Paris that you know?' he asked. Leroy didn't even lift his eyes from his book.

'I don't know any,' he replied. 'I know two lads in Little Ilford who go to dance classes, but that's for Latin American dancing.'

'Well . . . there you are. I won't have much competition from West Ham for a start. There won't be crowds at the audition and I can pick French up as I go along . . . most people do . . . so my Mum says.'

'They have unemployed people in France too you know. Unless you're a tap dancer they won't want to know about you.'

'I've got contacts over there,' Alan blurted out.

'Who?' challenged Leroy.

'Oh . . . er . . . Madame Louise . . . Monsieur Bari . . . and a German ballet dancer my Mum knows.' Alan turned away. Looking through the window again he saw that the two lights twinkling in the sky were getting brighter.

'And they're in show business in Paris?'

'Yes.'

'So when will you be going?'

'Well . . . after the exams. In the meantime I'm joining a dancing school.'

Leroy started to laugh. At first it wasn't much more than a suppressed chuckle but the clearer the picture of Alan Hogan at a dancing school became, the more laughter it provoked. Leroy fell off his chair and rolled about the floor in apparent agony.

Alan stood by the window, hurt and embarrassed by Leroy's hilarity. It was then that the significance of the two lights in the sky over the Thames occurred to him. As he watched they appeared to waver in the sky. It was about nine o'clock and on this blustery May evening the final streaks of day were being obliterated by heavy, gusting cloud. The two lights swayed alarmingly in the wind. There was no doubt about it. He could see the wings and the tail light. It was a small private aircraft.

'Just look at this . . . quick . . . quick Leroy!' he called. 'There's an aircraft coming over the docks.'

Leroy dropped his book and sprang to the window.

The plane banked and circled the Victoria Dock. They could see the pilot looking down. There didn't appear to be anything wrong with the engine. It throbbed healthily as it straightened out over the river and came in, dropping lower and lower.

'It can't land here,' Leroy said as he watched it anxiously from the window. 'The workmen haven't finished the site for the Stolport. There's no proper runway, it'll crash if it tries to land here!'

They watched as the small plane wavering in the wind butterflied down, till, with a final swooping dip, it landed on the soft shale of the new runway. It skipped lightly over the surface and after slowing down it revved its way towards the nearest shed. A van and two men emerged and unloaded some boxes from the plane into the van. Then an attachment was fixed to the plane and the van towed it towards Shed 22, the warehouse directly opposite the boys' hiding place. The plane was towed inside and after about twenty minutes the van drove away.

'I wonder what that's all about,' said Leroy. 'It can't be legal.'

'They're probably executives of the Development Corporation, storing things. One or two of these warehouses are let to private businesses now, you know.'

'Do you think we could rent out this office?' giggled Leroy.

'I wonder what's in them cases? They looked quite heavy,' said Alan. His curiosity was slowly asserting itself. It wasn't that he wanted to steal anything . . . just the tingling inquisitive desire to poke his nose into other people's business.

Leroy looked at his watch.

'It's only ten past nine. We could stroll round that way.' Leroy didn't mind having a peep into the shed either.

'It's a bit chancy . . . and it's dark over there!' Alan always attempted to persuade himself not to do something before he actually did it, particularly if the proposed course of action was dangerous, or, as in this case, illegal.

'Are you chicken?' Leroy smirked.

Alan thought for a moment.

'Yeh . . . I'm chicken.'

'What!' exclaimed Leroy.

'Yeh . . . I'm *chicken*,' he emphasised the word, 'all the time. My stomach churns over every time we climb through the fence to get here, and I'm really bloody chicken when I go to the clinic. What I'm good at is hiding it.'

'But if we walk over and take a look in that warehouse . . . you'll do it . . .'

'Oh yeh . . . I'll do it . . . but I'll be as scared as hell! I get no enjoyment out of doing these things . . . I only enjoy talking about them afterwards.' Alan smiled.

He really didn't mind admitting he was scared to Leroy. He'd seen the look of panic on Leroy's face once or twice when he was gasping for breath during an asthma attack.

'Well! Are you coming or not?' Leroy demanded.

'Yeh . . . I'm coming . . . I'm curious . . and I'm scared.'

They put the candles away. When their eyes got accustomed to the darkness they slowly felt their way down the steps to the dockside. It was still a blustery night, although the rain had stopped, and clouds scurried busily across the sky. Now and then the moon appeared and drew the deep, square shadows of the sheds on the water.

It took about ten minutes to walk round the basin to the other side. The PLA shed was the second in line from the dock Gate No. 2. There was an alleyway between it and the first shed.

'How do we get in?' Alan asked.

'Perhaps the shed has a back entrance,' Leroy replied.

They crept round the rear of the building. There was only one entrance and that was very difficult to negotiate. The back of this shed resembled the front of the shed where they had their hideout. An office, similar to the foreman's, was situated on the first floor with a window looking out onto the roadway towards the dock gate, but the iron stairway had collapsed and was lying rusting on the ground. The window of the office had been punched out by vandals and the remains of its wooden frame dangled down the corrugated iron sheets which boxed the shed.

'If we could climb up there . . . it would be simple to get in,' whispered Leroy.

Alan was getting cool about the whole idea. He kept looking round to make sure no one was following them.

'Look, Leroy . . . we can't get in. Let's just give it a miss. It's probably not worth the hassle anyway.'

'You are bloody chicken aren't you?' sneered Leroy.

'How do we get up there then, Oh brave and mighty!'

'Look,' Leroy said pointing at the rusting stairway. 'We prop it up at the side of the shed under the window and climb.'

'We can't lift that!' exclaimed Alan.

'Not all of it . . . it's broken anyway . . . there's the long bit with those plates stuck on the side of it where the steps used to be. Climbing that will be easy.'

Reluctantly Alan helped Leroy to disentangle the iron rail from the rest of the stairway. It made a terrible noise as bits fell off and clanged against the rest of the staircase. The noise echoed across the dock basin. Alan kept looking about him. He expected trouble any second.

They struggled with the rail and got it to lean against the side of the shed. It was about three feet short of the window.

'I'll go first,' Leroy volunteered.

He climbed quite nimbly at first but as he got higher the metal plates were missing and there were no footholds. His rubber-soled trainers, however, gave him just enough grip, enabling him to reach the windowsill. After two swinging attempts he sat astride the window ledge. He signalled Alan to follow.

Alan's heart was beating so loudly he could hear it. As he tentatively pressed his body against the steel rail and gripped the rusty plates for leverage he felt dizzy. Perspiration beaded his forehead and temples and he felt as if he were going to vomit. Half way up the rail he began to panic and looking up at Leroy he barely whispered the words, 'I can't make it . . . I'll have to . . . I'll have to . . .'

'Come on . . . you're just scared. When you get up here you'll be all right.' Leroy reached down. He clasped Alan's wrist. After a scramble, Alan got his leg over the windowsill and grabbed a steel support. A shower of rust trickled down. By now the dizziness had turned to a feeling of drowsiness. Leroy's voice seemed to be coming to him down a tunnel. His eyes couldn't focus and he felt very tired.

'I shouldn't have climbed . . . climbed . . . I shouldn't,' Alan said. His own voice seemed to be at a distance too. 'I've told . . . you . . . before . . . that climbing isn't any good for me . . . or my legs . . . for driving a BMW . . . BMW . . . driving . . . it's difficult . . . when . . . your legs . . . in a BMW and it's . . . them fellahs with the . . . my mother . . . said she . . . saw . . . in Paris . . . in . . . the . . .

in . . . the . . . in . . . the . . . spring . . . when . . . the . . . . BMW . . .' His voice trailed off into a mumble.

Leroy was perplexed but only for a moment. He remembered when they first met in the library during games periods that Alan had told him about his queer 'turns' when his blood sugar went funny. This must be one of them. It was whilst Leroy was working this out that Alan fell onto the grubby carpet and remained motionless. He appeared to be talking to himself.

Sitting on the floor beside him, Leroy levered Alan up into a sitting position. He slapped his face.

'Come on . . . come on, Alan.' He slapped his face again, but Alan looked at him as though he were a stranger. Leroy felt fear creep into his stomach just as Alan had described. Being faced with the dark side of your friend's disability for the first time can make anyone a bit panicky. Leroy started to talk aloud to himself partly in the hope that Alan would hear and reply.

'What the hell am I supposed to do? Alan, Alan!' he slapped his face again but there was no response. 'We're miles away from help here,' he shouted, 'and I can't run and leave you here on your own.' Then he remembered that Alan always carried a card. Quickly searching his pockets he found a plastic wallet and inside a card with Alan's photograph on it. It was too dark to read in the room and the candles were stored in their hiding place on the other side of the dock. He took the card to the window but he still couldn't make out the writing clearly. He remembered he'd pocketed two matches in the den. Normally he shaved them to points to use as tooth picks. Leroy was very proud of his teeth. He struck one of the matches but the breeze blew it out immediately; that's why they always put the candles in jam jars away from draughty places. He crouched down in the darkened corner of the room and struck the second match. It didn't flare up at first but Leroy held it within his cupped hands. It ignited properly and shielding it with his body he placed it over the card. It read:

> Alan Hogan
> Flat 58
> Silvertown Point
> Canning Town
> London, E7

I am a diabetic having daily insulin.

If I am found ill, please give me two spoonfuls of sugar, preferably in water, or a **glucose tablet** which you will find **in my pocket**. If I do not recover, **call a doctor or ambulance**.

Leroy searched Alan's pockets and found a metal tube of tablets. Alan was still mumbling as Leroy pushed a tablet into his mouth.

Nothing happened.

'If this doesn't work I'll have to get an ambulance,' Leroy thought.

Alan began to show signs of recovery. It was slow at first. His mouth moved and he mumbled. Slowly his breath began to alternate with a kind of sighing noise. Without warning his eyes started to focus.

'Oh . . . er . . . oh . . .'

'Alan . . . Alan . . . it's me, Leroy.'

'Who?'

'Leroy!'

'Yeh . . . I know you are Leroy. Have I had a hypo?'

'Well you've had something . . . it was like a half-faint . . . but I found your card and gave you a glucose tablet.'

'Oh . . . good. Give me another quick . . . I usually take two . . .'

Leroy passed him another tablet which Alan quickly crunched and swallowed.

'Just give it five minutes and I'll be all right. I didn't kick the furniture or anything did I?'

'There's nothing here to kick . . .'

'Sometimes I do silly things . . . but I don't know about them till I come out of it . . . I get a bit difficult . . . sort of awkward . . . but I feel all right now. I'll have to get home as quickly as I can and do a blood test . . . just to sort myself out . . . I've done everything I'm supposed to do . . . perhaps it was the cold wind and the excitement what did it.'

'And the climbing.'

'Yep . . . I suppose so.'

Leroy stood up and walked across the room to the place where the door used to be. He looked out.

'The inner stairs that lead down to the floor of the shed are all right. We could use them to save you climbing.'

Leroy tried the two top steps tentatively.

'And when we get to the bottom . . . what do we do? We'll still be inside the shed,' Alan asked wearily.

'I'll nip down and have a scout around,' Leroy said as he disappeared.

Alan didn't bother to get up. He just lay there with his back propped up against an old metal filing cabinet.

'That's the second one I've had this year,' he said to himself. 'The clinic said it might get a bit out of order . . . because of me age . . . now that I'm adolescent . . . whatever that is . . . I think it's the name parents give to difficult kids.' He made himself more comfortable 'Louise was an adolescent, so Mum said, when she threw all our cups through the window onto the concrete seventeen floors down. She threw that special mug I got from Rhyl with my name on it . . . it was the last thing Dad bought for me before . . .'

Alan's mind trailed off into a meandering daydream. He'd become very good at this daydreaming business. Although he supposed he'd always done it, it had become a kind of deliberate thing in recent years. When he felt a bit sorry for himself he just relaxed and let his mind take him for a pleasant inconsequential stroll into his fertile imagination. It was easy enough to do. It nearly always started with him imagining he was a success at something like rally driving, or that he'd won the pools. He'd frequently bought himself a house in the country and set up his Mum as housekeeper with servants to look after the place and cook the meals. There were horses in the stable – one of them had just won the Grand National – and several BMWs in the garage. After seeing the Boat Show on TV one night, he dreamed of buying a yacht in Brighton and taking a party of friends across to Dieppe for a meal. He always imagined Dieppe because he'd been on a trip there from the junior school and had tried to buy sweets in a shop speaking French. The lady in the shop asked him what he wanted in English so he didn't bother to use the phrases he'd rehearsed in class for weeks. Alan never believed in exerting himself unless it was absolutely necessary.

'If I owned this shed,' he thought to himself, 'I'd turn it into a huge games hall and rent it out every night to West Ham United for training. I'd be on first name terms with all the players and I'd automatically be a Director of the club with a regular seat in the stand.'

It was whilst he was deep in the throes of arriving in his Rolls Royce at the Wembley Cup Final that he heard the voices. Standing up slowly he crept to the door of the office. Peering into the darkness he saw two torch beams making their way along the opposite wall of the shed. The two torchbearers were talking. They stopped. The torches danced up and down the shed wall as if their owners were looking for something. After a little more conversation the torches altered direction. They were heading straight for the stairs leading to the office.

5

The End for Leroy

Leroy saw the torches too. He'd descended the stairway and made his way cautiously along the side of the shed looking for an opening. He didn't expect to find a convenient door but there was always the possibility that bits of sheeting had come away or had rusted and broken off leaving just enough space for two boys to squeeze through to the outside.

After about forty steps he stubbed his toe against a wooden spar . . . or that's what he thought it was. He reached out to remove it. His hand came into contact with a solid sheet of metal. Feeling his way he soon discovered that it was a dividing wall. When he came to its end he found he could walk round it. It was then that he stumbled into the packing cases. They seemed to be stacked quite high – ten feet perhaps – and covered in cloth of some kind. It was too dark to make out any marks or writing on the crates. He sat down on one of them to consider the position. It was still very dark and only the larger objects could be seen in outline. That's when he saw the torches.

A door at the end of the shed opened and the two torches came in. He saw them change direction and make for the stairs leading to the office where Alan was lying.

Perhaps it was some instinctive reaction that made him do it. Perhaps he'd seen some animal or bird on a TV nature programme create a diversion away from a defenseless or injured companion. It could have been a touch of the daredevil.

Leroy slipped off the crate and shouted 'Over here, mate . . . I'm over here!' He dashed away as fast as the darkness would permit. He bumped into wooden objects and banged his shins on a metal rack, creating a lot of noise, and fuss. The two torchlights switched in his direction but he was too far away for them to illuminate him in any detail. What light they did provide enabled Leroy to see a little more of his immediate environment and helped him to avoid the larger objects. As the torches swung about the walls searching for him, he lay flat on the floor, so as not to present a shadow on the wall behind. As the beam passed overhead and swung quickly to his right he glimpsed what appeared to be a small door to another office, built at ground floor level in the corner of the shed. By now he could hear the men's voices. They were getting nearer and the torch beams were much brighter. Waiting for a dark patch between himself and the office door he ran and crouched by the door and waited once more for the torch beams to pass. Reaching up, he palmed the door handle, very gently pulled it down and eased the door open. Taking a quick glance in the direction of the torches he stood up and squeezed himself through the door, partly closing it silently behind him.

The torches met and appeared to be talking. After a few moments one of the torches moved off in the direction of the exit where the boys had seen the men unloading the van earlier in the evening. It took the man about three minutes to walk to the exit. A few seconds later lights began to appear all around the shed. A man in a navy blue boiler suit was systematically pulling the switches, and strips of light were illuminating the shed's cargo bays.

Leroy squinted, one-eyed, through a crack in the door. He saw the light aircraft standing near the exit. It was a high-winged monoplane, quite small, capable of carrying a pilot and three passengers. It was very similar to the small flying club aircraft he'd seen at Stapleford Abbey Flying Club out in Essex where he went with his uncle on Sunday afternoons. It was painted white with a red stripe down the side and a red tail fin.

The real surprise, however, was a huge, fat fishing boat secured by thick, white ropes to bollards mounted in the centre of the shed. The concrete floor beneath it had been taken out to form a ramp which sloped towards the side of the shed. A section of the shed's corrugated iron sheeting had been removed and huge wooden doors substituted. By standing up, Leroy could see water lapping under the bottom of the doors. It was a slip launch for the boat, leading out into the dock. Beneath the office in which Alan was hiding was a powerful engine and winch. It was used to pull the boat (or boats) out of the dock. The boat's single mast was laid across its deck from bow to midships and a small cabin, similar to that of an inshore fishing vessel, filled the stern and housed the wheel.

The remaining portion of the shed was divided into bays, most of which contained labelled crates of various shapes and sizes. From those bays nearest to Leroy, there was a strong smell of tobacco. It looked an ordered and business-like place. There was nothing derelict about this warehouse. The surprise of these revelations absorbed his attention. That's why he never saw the arm that reached through the office window behind him and grabbed him round the throat.

Alan watched the torches approaching the stairway. The derelict office provided no hiding place. There was no question of him attempting to climb down the metal stair propped up outside the window. He'd have to give himself up and explain they were just curious, he wasn't feeling too well and could they please go home. He'd get a good telling off from his Mum; their hiding place would become public knowledge; there might be a court case for trespass. Well, it didn't matter much. They were caught and that was that.

He stood in the doorway looking down at the outline of the staircase. As the torches approached he could see the staircase a little more clearly. He gripped the door for support. It was at that moment that Leroy called out. The torches swung away and began to follow him. Alan knew immediately how Leroy would expect him to behave. This was now a game. A game for two players. The diversion was to enable him to secure his position and when the searchers were nearing Leroy he would divert them in Alan's direction and confuse them.

Alan crept quickly down the staircase and hid behind a group of packing cases. The two torchbearers were now almost at the rear wall of the shed. He too saw them confer and then separate. Alan thought for a moment. They obviously hadn't got Leroy yet so there was no need to decoy them away. He would wait to see their next move.

When the lights started to come on, Alan was equally dumbfounded by the appearance of the boat from the darkness. As the lights came on above him he ducked down. Peering around the edge of a case he spotted a tall man in a boiler suit carrying a torch in one hand and looking towards an office in the far corner of the shed. He watched him move cautiously towards it. He was about to stand up and create his diversionary shout when he saw another man running down the shed from behind the boat. He was also wearing a boiler suit and an American style baseball cap with a large peak. He was carrying a gun.

The shout dried in Alan's throat. He watched, paralysed with shock, as the first man grabbed Leroy and held him till the second man arrived. Leroy's shouts and the men's grunts as they struggled to control him echoed round the vastness of the shed. A quick movement from the second man and a small cracking sound and Leroy slumped to the floor. The men looked at him. One of them knelt down beside him and turned him over.

'He's only a kid . . . a bloody kid.'

'Oh, God! Now what? What the hell are we going to do with him?'

'This could foul up the whole business.'

'Let's get him down to the van and get instructions on the 'phone.'

'What a bloody mess!'

They lifted Leroy and carried him down to the exit. He was unconscious . . . or was he? Alan's stomach turned over. Could he be dead? Had they killed him in the struggle?

Alan made his way cautiously down his side of the shed. As he drew parallel with the boat he saw a white bird painted on its prow and the word 'Tregammon' in white letters above it. He dashed from one of the bays and hid behind a large green crate.

The men laid Leroy down on a pile of old sacks by the sliding doors. One man stayed beside him whilst his companion in the baseball cap went to the van. Alan could just see him open the rear door, reach inside and bring out a portable telephone. Pulling out the aerial he dialled a number. After a few minutes' conversation he came back to where his mate was watching Leroy. All Alan heard was the man in the baseball cap saying,

'That's what he said. We'll never get away with this . . . its ridiculous!'

'If that's the order, that's what we do. He's the boss.'

They began to drag Leroy outside. They propped him up by one of the old dockside bollards used in the old days for securing ships to the dock wall. Then they turned the lights off and each took a side of the tall, heavy sliding doors and shut them. Alan heard them put a chain and padlock on the door. There was a bit of conversation which he couldn't make out now the doors were shut. Chains were rattled and dragged along the dockside, then silence. After a couple of minutes there was a loud splash. There was a little more conversation then someone got in the van, started it up and drove away.

Alan was about to make his way to the door when he heard footsteps outside. There was somebody walking up and down the dockside. Perhaps only one man had gone in the van. There was no escape in that direction. In fact, at that moment there was no escape in any direction except back the way he'd come, up the stairway and out through the window. It was too dark inside the shed. He'd never find his way back there without creating a noise.

He fumbled his way back to the nearest bay and sat down behind a crate to think things out. As his mind replayed the scenes of the last half hour, a slow, terrifying sequence forced itself into his imagination. It was easy to recall the scenes he'd witnessed: the torches flashing, the lights coming on, the men appearing and struggling with Leroy, the telephone message and the closing of the doors. It was at this point that an appalling scenario unfolded before him. The men dragged Leroy to the edge of the dock. They tied chains to his feet. Then they threw him into the dock. The splash. That splash could only be Leroy being thrown in. They'd drowned Leroy. They'd killed him.

6

A Tight Spot

Alan was up against it. No matter which way you looked at the facts, Alan was in a fix.

His mind was a blur of half impressions and as one thought chased another he lost track of the sequence. He couldn't make much sense of anything he had seen or heard except the one terrible fact that Leroy had been murdered. Every time he visualised the scene he stiffened with fear. That sharp cracking sound, the body slumping to the floor. Had they broken his neck with a commando grip, snapping his spine like matchwood? The perspiration trickled down past Alan's ear and dripped from his chin. The splashing sound in the dock recurred time and time again . . . he wished he could switch off the thoughts that returned to plague him. He began to shake. He clasped his knees together to prevent them vibrating. His whole body shook. His mouth dried and he suddenly became aware of the coldness in his feet and calves.

He heard the footsteps outside again. They stopped. The sound of a striking match. In the distance he heard East Ham Town Hall clock striking. Looking at his watch, he pressed the button which illuminated the display. It was 10 o'clock. He wouldn't be missed till around 11 o'clock. Mum and Louise didn't worry about him when he was out with Leroy. They liked him a lot. Marcia was quietly pleased that he'd found a friend who was sensible, and Louise smiled at him and gave him plenty of attention.

It always puzzled Alan that grown-ups could be quite

wrong about people. It was true that Leroy was sensible and reliable, but he was also crafty, secretive and quite mischievous when he wanted to be. Of course Mum would blame Alan for the whole thing. Leroy would be the innocent victim of one of his silly ideas. It would be *his* fault that Leroy was dead and yet it had all been Leroy's idea in the first place.

Alan's mind blurred again. It did occur to him that perhaps he hadn't fully recovered from his hypo. Wouldn't it be wonderful if he suddenly woke up and discovered he had had a really bad one and it was all a dream? He ran his fingers over the sacking surrounding the crate he was hiding behind. It was rough and real. This was no dream.

'If you ever get into a tight spot,' Dad had said to him once when they were at Maldon, 'sit down and try to work it out slowly by talking to yourself.' Dad had spoken quite a bit to Alan that summer two years ago. Perhaps he'd been preparing him for the break up that was to come. 'Just talk to yourself, and you'll be surprised how things will sort themselves out,' he'd insisted. Anything was worth a try in his predicament. Where should he begin?

'Well,' he said aloud to himself, 'this is a mess . . . a bloody awful mess. We came here . . . just out of curiosity . . . intending no harm to man or property . . . there's nothing here to nick . . . I wouldn't know what to do with the plane . . .' A little smile twisted the corner of his mouth. 'Then they caught Leroy and . . .' His mind jumbled again as though deliberately trying to turn his thoughts back, back again to Leroy's killing. 'OK . . . well, let's face it then,' he muttered. 'They killed Leroy . . . and . . . if they get me . . .they'll kill me too. Why? Why should they kill anyone for what's in this shed?

What's so important that people must be killed if they've seen the plane and the boat . . . or was it a mistake? Did they think that Leroy was somebody else . . . some enemy . . . some agent? Was it the boxes and the crates?'

He turned to the crate he was leaning against. It had the usual customs marks and code numbers on one side. Removing a bit of the sacking that partly covered the casing he peered round the other side. 'Leewarden Valcheran, Netherlands' was burnt in brown letters across its middle. Whatever it contained it looked as though it had come from Holland. The crate smelt of tobacco. A white label was stapled to the upper surface. His head almost touching the wood, Alan made out the name and address printed there. It read 'Murchison and Drew, Maldon, Essex'. That was opposite where Dad kept his boat, he thought. Perhaps the contents were connected with the coastal trade they operated on that wharf.

The footsteps returned. They stopped by the door. The chain rattled and he heard a single click followed by the chain falling to the floor. Whoever was outside had cut the chain. The door opened. It opened very slowly and in a jerky fashion. The person wasn't very strong, and he could hear them panting with the exertion. When the door had opened about a metre the pushing stopped. Alan watched the opening. A figure entered the shed. The person reached up to a switch by the door and two lights came on. Standing near the sacking where Leroy had lain was a woman. She was quite tall, about 5ft 10ins, wearing a white mac and a scarf tied round her head. Her hair emerged from the scarf and formed a fringe almost to her eyebrows. The hair was very blond, almost white blond. She wore dark socks and flat-heeled shoes. Because the lighting was immediately above, her features were in heavy shadow but as she moved towards the plane her face became clearer. She had pointed features and on her cheek near her nose there was a small cyst. Alan recognised it because Louise had developed a similar growth and had been so upset that Dad had paid for her to have it removed at a beauty clinic. It wasn't as big as the one Louise had cried about, but it was plainly visible.

The woman strolled to the aircraft, took a notebook from her pocket and, looking at the instrument panel, she made a few notes. Alan heard the sound of a car approaching. It stopped. Two men appeared in the doorway. The elder man was very tall, dressed like a seaman and wearing large rubber boots. It was the man he'd seen sitting in the back of Connie's BMW. His companion was smaller, blond and wearing jeans and an anorak. The woman in the white mac got down from the cockpit and after a brief conversation they all went to the fishing boat. The elder man climbed aboard whilst the woman walked towards the wooden doors that guarded the slipway. She pressed a button and with a bang and a clatter the doors began to open. The blond lad jumped down and began to grease the slipway and after a couple of minutes he retreated to the engine room which operated the winch.

It was only then that the advantages of the situation dawned on Alan. He was completely out of sight; the door was open. Could he chance the run of fifty or sixty yards to the door? Would they suddenly appear at the prow of the boat, take out a revolver and shoot him as he was silhouetted by the lights? If he stayed where he was he'd be caught anyway. He decided to chance it. He counted to three . . . one . . . two . . . three . . . and shot out from behind the packing cases straight for the door. He never looked left or right. It seemed miles to the door. If they saw him would he feel a bullet in his flesh? He ran faster than he'd ever run before and in seconds he was out into the night air. Sprinting down the dockside he never looked back. Two cars were parked near Gate No. 2. They were empty.

'That's their cars,' Alan thought as he scurried around the . . . and made his way between Sheds 22 and 23.

Squeezing between the wooden sleepers of the fence he crossed the railway line and ducked under the barbed wire. As he approached the hut occupied by the security man on Gate No. 1 he saw two figures inside. One was standing and holding a mug in his hand and the other sitting, answering the telephone.

'That's what I want,' he muttered, 'that telephone. I must tell the police what's happened . . . about Leroy.'

He saw the man put down the 'phone. The door of the hut opened and he walked out and leaned on the barrier, looking down the dock road towards Canning Town. A van approached. It stopped and a man in a boiler suit got out and spoke to the security guard. The guard pointed towards the hut. The man in the boiler suit went inside and picked up the 'phone. By the light inside the hut Alan recognised him as one of the men who had murdered Leroy, the one who had grabbed him round the neck. The security guards seemed to know him. When he put the phone down he grinned and nodded to the security guard who offered him a mug of tea. The man came out of the hut and jumped into the van. The guard lifted the rail and the van drove through. It was on its way back to the shed where the plane and the boat were housed. If the inquisitive woman wasn't sharp eared and alert she'd probably get the same treatment as Leroy. There'd be no point asking to use the security guard's 'phone. They'd never believe his story. Perhaps they were all part of the same gang.

Alan approached the hut cautiously. He waited until the guard who had raised the barrier had returned to the hut. The door shut behind him. Alan crept forward to the corner of the hut. He could hear their radio playing pop music. Bending double he tiptoed past the door and beneath the window. He negotiated the space next to the barrier's counter balance. He was out on the road. He crossed over and paused in the shadow cast by the wooden gates that led round the back of the Hat and Feather. The brewery lorries used these gates which led to a cobbled courtyard, giving them easy access to the pub's cellars. Alan looked back. There was no sign of the security men.

All the pub lights were on. The Hat and Feather was a popular pub, a meeting place for the boxing crowd who had a gymnasium and training facilities on the first floor and the bowling club whose club house and bowling green were situated at the back with an entrance from the cobbled courtyard where Alan was resting. His Dad had been interested in the big bowls matches and Alan had been taken there a couple of times.

Satisfied that he wasn't being followed, he made his way to the 'phone box on the corner opposite the pub. Closing the door he lifted the receiver and dialled 999. He waited. Nothing happened. He replaced the receiver and dialled again. There was no clicking noise or any indication that the 'phone was in order. Glancing down he saw that somebody had rammed coins into the slits and bent them so that nobody could get their money in. He noticed then that the receiver wasn't connected. The cord was snapped off. The 'phone was useless. Turning to push open the door, he saw a Lancia sports car drive into the courtyard behind the pub. A woman got out. It was the mystery woman he'd just seen in the shed. She locked the car and entered the pub from the back entrance. The car was a B registration model.

'She must have come the long way round from Gate No. 1,' Alan thought. Who were these people? They seemed to be able to come and go as they pleased.

A bus pulled up outside the pub. Alan sprinted across the road and got on it.

'Canning Town Library,' he said.

'Right, son,' the driver said giving him change from his 50p piece.

The bus had two passengers downstairs; an old lady in a black overcoat with two shopping bags that filled the seat beside her, and a man. In his agitated state of mind Alan didn't glance at either of them. He sat down and absent-mindedly looked out of the window at the new housing estate and the amber street lights. He didn't see them at all. His mind was racing, trying to make sense of the evening's terrifying events. He should have gone into the pub and told somebody. Perhaps they would have 'phoned the police. But if he'd gone in there and been seen by the woman in the Lancia she would have . . .

At that moment his eyes focused on the reflection in the bus window of the man in the seat across the gangway. The man was wearing an anorak over a boiler suit and as Alan watched him he took a cap from the seat beside him and put it on his head. It was an American baseball cap.

Alan gripped the seat in front to steady his nerves. He used the bus window to take a good look at the man. The police would want a detailed description so if he could concentrate this would help them to bring the killer to justice. Alan estimated his age at about 28 or 30. He was well-built, muscular, broad-backed, a heavy man. His hair was cut short, giving him a military appearance, and he was wearing black boots. He sat upright in the bus seat and whistled. Alan couldn't make out the tune. It wasn't in the Top 20 whatever it was.

As the bus approached Canning Town Alan began to think of his next step. Ought he to go straight to the police station? Somehow the idea wasn't very attractive. He'd never been in a police station before and the place looked so forbidding from the outside. It wasn't the kind of place you called in for a chat and policemen were formidable and threatening people. The sight of their uniform always meant trouble for somebody. Alan, when he thought about it, had never spoken to a policeman in the whole of his life and most people avoided them in Canning Town.

Alan noticed the bus had changed direction. Road repairs had forced the driver to make a detour. The bus would now pass within a hundred yards of Silvertown Point. He could dash home and tell Louise and his mother. They would do the rest. He stood up and positioned himself near the driver. In the 'pay as you board' buses you could chat to the driver.

'Could you drop me off on the next corner. I didn't know you'd be coming this way,' Alan said. The driver looked at him and smiled.

'I didn't know myself, son. It's a burst water main I think . . . they want it done before the morning or there'll be traffic chaos on that road.' He slowed the bus to a stop. 'Now, son, will this do?'

The driver opened the doors. Alan jumped down and waited for the bus to continue before crossing the road. The man in the baseball cap was still sitting on the lower deck. When the road was clear Alan sprinted across and dashed down the short cul-de-sac that led to Silvertown Point. He pressed the button for the lift. The indicator showed that it was four floors up. He heard the lift gates close. The lift hummed down and the doors juddered open. Stepping in he pressed button seventeen.

I'll tell Louise and then she can use Mrs Cartwright's 'phone,' he muttered to himself. As the doors opened he had the key to the flat ready in his hand. Inserting it quickly he flung open the door and dashed in shouting, 'Louise, Louise where are you?' There was no reply. He looked into the kitchen. It was empty.

'Louise!' he called again. He walked into the lounge. There was a man sitting in the lounge chair by the TV. His Dad stood up and said, 'Hey, Alan! Thought I'd call round and see how you were. There's nobody in. They've left a message.'

Alan ran to him and much to Fred's surprise flung his arms around him and burst into tears.

7

Dad Helps Out

Fred sat the lad down.

'Now listen, Alan. Just stop blabbing and start from the beginning. I can't make any sense of what you're saying.' The sight of his father had somehow released all the emotions that had been bottled up inside Alan.

'Start from the beginning. You and Leroy went to the docks this evening. OK. Now, what happened next?'

Slowly and patiently Fred helped him to recount the tale. When it came to the part about Leroy, Alan started to cry again.

Fred went into the kitchen and put the kettle on. When he came back he placed an arm around Alan.

'Come on, Alan. We'll sort it all out.'

'You'd better ring the police, Dad. We want them on to the job as soon as possible so that they can be nicked.'

'True . . . true,' Dad said but he didn't seem in any great hurry to do it at the moment.

'You can use Mrs Cartwright's 'phone upstairs,' Alan said.

'Now just a minute, son. There's proper ways of doing everything. Now listen. You go and clean yourself up and put some clean clothes on. You could do with a bath the state you're in. Then do your blood test – make sure the excitement hasn't upset you too much – and in the meantime I'll sort things out. I'll nip out to a 'phone box. I don't want to bother her upstairs, she's deaf anyway. Now, go on into the bathroom and run yourself a hot bath. I'll sort it all out.'

'But you'll ring the police and tell 'em?'

'Just as soon as I can get to the 'phone. I'll use the one at the Beckton Arms. Now, don't worry, son.'

Alan went into the bathroom and turned on the taps for a bath. Gazing into the mirror he got a shock. His hair was full of bits of straw and there was a series of scratches down his left cheek. His hands were filthy, stained brown with the rust, and his thumb was cut. The blood had congealed and bits of sacking were stuck to it. He was pale and red-eyed. He was a mess.

Lying in the bath he looked at the pile of clothes he'd dumped on the floor. He must have looked a sight. Why hadn't the people on the bus noticed? Too preoccupied with their own thoughts? Thank heavens the man in the baseball cap hadn't noticed either.

He heard the door to the flat close. He presumed Dad was on his way to inform the police. The traumas of the evening didn't predispose Alan to lie in his bath luxuriating in its warmth. He just wanted to get clean. He scrubbed his body as though cleansing himself of the whole messy, dirty business. As he dried himself with the bath towel he remembered his blood test. Having put on his bath robe he reached for his plastic box and took out the special needle for pricking the finger. Placing his hand palm upwards on the table by the wash basin he quickly prodded the needle into the soft flesh of his finger tip. He squeezed his finger until a bulb of blood was balanced precariously on the tip. Taking a thin test strip from a tube he gently lowered the globule of blood onto the coloured section on the end. He timed it on his watch for sixty seconds and then removed the blood. He waited another sixty seconds to see what shade of blue the chemical on the test strip became. On the side of the test strip container was a series of colour codes. Alan compared his test strip with the code and decided he was a little low in blood sugar. Perhaps the excitement and the exercise had affected him more than usual. He popped a couple of glucose tablets into his mouth.

The hot bath had helped him relax. The warmth of the bath robe and the central heating made him feel a little sleepy. He walked over to the TV and switched it on. After flicking over the channels with the remote control, he settled for snooker. It was an early round of a major tournament. Jimmy White was giving an over-anxious newcomer from South Africa a lesson in the art of break-making.

He picked up a note on top of the TV. It read, 'Alan, Mum and I are going to the cinema. Back about 11.15. Love Louise.'

Dad still had a key to the flat. He wondered if Mum realised that. It was the first time he could remember his

Dad turning up unexpectedly like this. Perhaps he'd finished with his girlfriend and wanted to come back. He couldn't imagine Mum or Louise allowing that.

Alan loved his father. He could remember lots of happy times they'd spent together, days out at Southend, football on the beach, trips to the pantomime at the Stratford Theatre Royal and being taken to see a boxing match at the Albert Hall. He'd been to Earl's Court for the Boat Show and when the diabetes came along his Dad took him to Romford Road Baths for swimming lessons so that he could have a regular form of exercise as recommended by the doctors. That was the year he felt closest to his father.

He also remembered the dark side of Fred, the stories his mother told about the early days of their marriage. He'd had a regular job as a clerk in the works department of the local council. It wasn't well paid but they'd saved enough between them to put down the deposit on a flat. Louise had been born and then Alan. Marcia's Grandma died and left them a bit of money from a house in Bolton. It only raised a few thousand but it was enough to put a deposit on a house in Plaistow, a nice, three-bedroomed terraced house in a good street with nice neighbours.

Fred became dissatisfied with his job. He felt he could do better but he wasn't sure what he'd be better at. One night a friend invited him to Romford dog track. He backed a treble – three winners – and came home with £800 in his pocket. It changed his life. He started his 'schemes'. The whisky job and his alibi ruined everything.

They were all shattered by this sequence of events. From being a happy, cosy, loving family they'd been reduced to genteel poverty and a council flat in Canning Town.

He was so plausible. As Marcia said, it was an illness

without any obvious symptoms. It wasn't like booze where everyone could see that you were a drunk. This urge to make a 'quick buck' was insidious. He was always apologetic. He cried. Then he'd tell them about another of his 'schemes'. 'Today I could have cracked it . . . if Lester had done the business for me. £500 . . . and he let me down . . . I had a nice little earner lined up for that cash.'

Marcia got the flat in Silvertown Point and banned him from it. She relented when he pleaded with her to give him another chance. She forgave Biddy Sullivan – she reckoned she was a mental case but after a month he was at it again. One night he came home drunk and tried to drag Marcia into their bedroom. They shouted and swore at each other. Next door banged on the wall and told them to grow up. Fred grabbed Louise – she was fourteen – and said,

'Well, if you won't . . . she will.'

Marcia picked up a chair and knocked him unconscious. The ambulance came and a statement was made to the police but they heard no more about it. Fred wrote a letter apologising, but he never received a reply. Marcia started the divorce proceedings that week.

Alan couldn't think of any circumstances in which Marcia and Louise would tolerate living with him again. As sometimes happens in these affairs, Fred eventually *did* have the luck he'd always prophesied. He had a sequence of big wins and bought himself a bungalow in Maldon which he shared with his current girlfriend.

He was great fun at holiday time but they always had the feeling he was glad when the it was over. Perhaps the memories of his past were too painful for him to think about them for long periods. He never remembered their birthdays, but Alan loved him just the same. Whenever he thought about him he could remember times when he was frightened of the dark when he was in bed and his Dad came upstairs, rubbed his tummy and told his stories or sang songs. 'We ain't got a barrel of money, Maybe we're ragged and funny, But we'll travel along, Singing a song, Side by Side.' Alan fell asleep slumped in front of the telly.

His Dad woke him.
'Come on, Alan . . . pack your things . . . you're coming with me to Maldon.'
'What?'
'You're coming to Maldon . . . just for the weekend.'
'What for?'
'I've been advised by the police. They think you ought to have a bit of peace and quiet for a couple of days. Go on now. Get your clothes together.'
'Are the police on to them? The killers?'
'They'll be down there now I should imagine.'
'But won't they want to speak to me? I saw it all. I could help them identify the men . . . and the woman.'
'Not necessary at this stage, they say. Perhaps Monday.'
'Why must I go to Maldon?'
'Police think it would be safer . . . for you.'
'Safe . . . why, who'd have a go at me? Nobody saw me.'
'They're a very clever gang, the police reckon. As soon as it hits the papers it's bound to get out that Leroy had a mate and that he, most likely, witnessed the whole thing. Then it's only a few days before the gang finds out who it was and where you live. They'll probably ask at school . . . ask your mates at school. They're very clever when their lives are at stake. They'll want you snuffed out. So just go to your bedroom. Get packed and I'll leave a note for your mother.'

'Why can't the police protect me here?'

'Well, it's not just the police . . . it's the press as well. They'd crowd round the flats, taking photographs and asking questions. You know what it's like. You've seen it on TV dozens of times. They invade your home and then write lies about you. Come on, don't argue.'

'If I come back here on Monday all that will happen anyway, won't it?'

'Look. If the police don't clear up this business by Monday they may insist on you remaining in Maldon. Now come on, do that packing.'

Alan reluctantly began to fill one of his mother's cases with shirts and underclothes. His Dad took his overcoat and a spare pair of shoes and went down and put them in his car. When he came back Alan was almost ready.

'Have you got your insulin stuff and the needles?' his Dad asked.

Alan went into the bathroom and placed all his medicine and equipment into a waterproof holdall. Louise had bought it for him for his last birthday.

'I'll not be a minute, Dad,' Alan called from the bathroom. He closed the door and locked it.

'What are you doing?'

'I'm taking a blood test,' he lied. Alan really wanted a few moments to think things out. He was still drowsy after falling asleep on the sofa. He had this feeling. He couldn't quite put his finger on it. Every story, TV play or report in the paper that involved somebody being killed had a scene in it where the major witness was interviewed by the police. On the *Police Five* programme they spent nearly all of their time asking for key witnesses. Why should the police ignore him and suggest he go into hiding? Perhaps they knew all about it already and didn't want any complications. His imagination went into overdrive. He could see himself being kidnapped by the gang and being held for ransom. His mother, told not to tell the police, was asking Gary to sell three BMWs for the money. His photo was in the paper and Louise was interviewed on TV and crying in front of the camera.

'Let him go!' she cried out. 'Let him go and then he can return to the bosom of his family!'

His Dad knocked on the door.

'Have you finished yet? We'll have to get cracking. I've left a note for your mother.'

'OK . . . just a minute.' The mention of a note for his mother gave him an idea. He took a small tissue from his blood-testing kit and wrote a note to Louise with one of her eye-brow pencils.

'Saw Leroy killed in docks. Dad has rung police. Gone to Maldon with Dad. Alan.'

He propped it up on the small cupboard above the sink unit.

8

The Secret of the Wardrobe

Alan was quite surprised by the C registration Mercedes Coupe his Dad had acquired.

The drive to Maldon was uneventful. Fred drove more slowly than usual: he was deep in thought. Normally he tried to engage Alan in hearty conversation as if trying to make up to his children for not seeing them for long periods. He'd tell jokes and thump Alan's arm when it came to the funny bits. Alan was expected to roar his head off, but he never did. He could never understand why his Dad laughed at such stupid stories. Alan noticed too that Fred frequently retold the same stories, each subsequent telling more elaborate than the last. One of his stories concerned Bertie Shaw, a friend of his, who played a violin but whose real job was blowing up derelict buildings and chimneys. As the story developed Dad would maintain that Bertie played the violin every time he blew up a chimney but Alan knew he never did, so what was the point?

They took the Chelmsford bypass and after a few miles they turned off onto the road through the hill village of Danbury. This was the part of the journey Alan always enjoyed. Living in London he didn't get much opportunity to see things from the top of a hill. He remembered a visit when he was in the infant school to Parliament Hill Fields in North London. He'd been fascinated by the view over London – St Paul's Cathedral, the new skyscrapers in the City, the Post Office Tower. Dad had shown Louise how to fly a kite, a box kite in red and yellow. Alan remembered looking at the kite and wondering what kept it up in the sky and how wonderful it must be to be up so high, looking down on everything. The kite, he thought, always looked sad and deflated when it was pulled down by his father. It lay on the grass, flat and inert, a lifeless thing, not the weaving, bobbing, laughing object he'd seen in the sky. A bit like life with Dad, he thought – one moment it's excitement and joy and the next everything falls flat and you're destitute, broke, out in the street.

Even in the dark the hill at Danbury gave a wonderful view of the Essex flat lands and the lines of roadway lights like strings of yellow beads joining the towns and villages together, holding each other's hands for comfort in the dark night. A train, like an illuminated caterpillar, slowly nosed its way towards Southend across the black marsh.

Cresting the hill the car probed the dark lanes towards Maldon. There wasn't much to see at night, just a group of house lights in the distance beyond the town. Two or three navigation lights flickered on the River Blackwater, a couple of fishing boats steering out into the North Sea.

They arrived at the bungalow at about 12.30. Dad got out and opened the front door whilst Alan undid the boot and got out his luggage. Another car turned into the driveway behind Fred's car. It was a BMW. Alan recognised it at once as the one belonging to Connie Masters, Dad's latest. Alan didn't want to speak to her just now. The effort of making polite conversation was beyond him. He took his bags into the hall.

'Same room as last time, Dad?' he shouted.

'Yeh . . . front room on the right, son.' Dad replied.

Alan shouldered the door open and threw his bags onto the single bed. The room was small but comfortable. The single bed was covered with a yellow and white floral duvet. Beside the bed was a small, white chest of drawers on which was placed a red reading lamp. The small gas radiator was turned on low beneath the window so the room was pleasantly warm. A large oak wardrobe filled the wall opposite the window. It had been purchased secondhand at a sale in Bartlingham Hall the summer before Alan remembered the trouble they'd had getting it through the doors and the narrow hallway into this room. In fact the wardrobe had been intended for the main bedroom at the back of the house but it was too large to manoeuvre through the kitchen.

Alan unpacked quite slowly. He was still a bit fuzzy from the hypo. Sometimes after one of these attacks he recovered quite quickly but on other occasions, and this appeared to be one of them, he'd need a day or two to get over it properly. He slipped a glucose tablet into his mouth. He'd do a blood test before getting into bed just to check that the day's excitement hadn't altered his blood sugar levels too much. He'd been warned that things might get difficult as he got older because he was growing fast. His body would have trouble adjusting if his body chemistry was normal, but with the complication of diabetes he had to check and double check, particularly after a hypo.

He opened the wardrobe door and began putting his two jackets and his pullovers onto coat hangers. Alan liked to dress well even though he had limited cash. What he had was good quality and well looked after. He had an Italian wool pullover that was worth £40 – he got it for £27 in Stratford Market – but he always told everybody it really cost £60. His jeans were stonewashed Levis and his socks were bought in Dieppe on the school trip. He admired any garment that had a foreign label. His shoes were from Marks and Spencers but he cracked on, as they were Spanish leather, that an Aunt had got them in Majorca. Whenever he felt the need for clothes he'd volunteer to clean the cars at Gary's garage. Gary was very lazy about cleaning the cars so he was grateful for the help and showed his appreciation in the normal way – with cash.

Placing his brown shoes on the rack at the bottom of the wardrobe Alan remembered that when Louise and he had first used it they'd explored the inside. The wardrobe was probably nearly two hundred years old and had been made for a rich country squire and his family. They'd discovered that the cupboard had a false bottom and by removing the shoe rack and placing two fingers through a gap beneath it you could remove a piece of oak about a foot square. They speculated that perhaps at some time in the past the wardrobe had been part of a lady's bedroom furniture and this was her secret hiding place for her jewel box. Well, that was Alan's story and Louise went along with it because she quite liked the idea of being associated with a very wealthy person from the past. Neither of them had met anyone who was very wealthy although they'd seen such people on TV programmes. They'd watched a programme one wet evening about a country house in the Cotswolds. The house had twenty bedrooms and a Great Hall full of statues and works of art. One of the pictures in the dining room was worth £500,000 and a pair of silver candlesticks had been valued at £20,000. The house and grounds were worth millions of pounds and as the camera panned back into the helicopter, giving the viewers an aerial view, Louise turned to Alan and sighed.

'I wish we lived in a place like that.'

'But the fellah says he can't afford to keep it! It costs so much to run it. We couldn't pay the heating bills. Just think, every time it needed painting it would cost a fortune.'

'I wonder how they got it in the first place?' Louise mused.

'His Dad died and left it to him . . . his Dad was a General in India.'

'Wouldn't it be nice though?'

'It doesn't look a homely sort of place to me. This flat isn't much but it's comfortable . . . you can wrap the place around you. When you look at their lounge, it's big, the furniture's big, the space between things is big and you'd always be frightened of knocking something over in case it cost fifty thousand quid to replace. And all them visitors on Sundays. Just as you felt like a mug of tea and a piece of fruit cake all these people'd walk through and look at you as though you were goldfish in a bowl.'

'Just imagine lying on that carpet,' Louise had that far away look on her face. 'Warming yourself in front of a log fire after coming home on a cold wet day from a trip to Harrods. The butler putting tea and muffins on a tray to bring in. And look at the walls . . . they don't have them stupid plaster ducks flying up into the ceiling or tatty wallpaper with dark damp patches showing through. And they don't have neighbours who nick the milk or dogs that pee in the lifts.'

'Well, they're rich. They can afford anything. You never know. Dad might make a packet on the dogs.'

'And pigs might fly!' snorted Louise.

Alan reached down and took out the rail on the shoe rack. He lifted the oak panel. Somebody had lined the cavity with thick brown paper. There was a container in it the size of a shoe box and made from a hard plastic material. It was coloured bright orange and had a hook moulded into one end. The lid was held on with three metal clips that showed signs of rust. Flicking the clips open Alan lifted the lid. Packed neatly in three piles were hundreds of ten pound notes. Alan looked at them. He put out his hand and gently ran his fingers across the surface of the notes. It looked and felt like real money. Fred must have had another big win. Alan couldn't count the notes in his confusion. Coming into contact with so much money was such a strange event that he had no appropriate behaviour for dealing with it. He heard someone filling a kettle in the kitchen. It broke his dream-like trance and he quickly replaced the lid and closed the secret panel. He placed his shoes, heels up, on the rack. Sitting on the bed he changed into his trainers.

'There must be at least a couple of thousand pounds in there,' he thought as he tied his laces. 'You could do a lot with two thousand quid. You could get a good second-hand car for that. Not a BMW of course. Mum could have that holiday in Paris, look up old friends like Madame Louise and me and Leroy . . .'

The thought of Leroy screwed him up inside. The brief respite of thinking about the money had allowed him to relax from the tension of Leroy's death. Alan lay back on the bed. For the hundredth time he replayed the events of the early evening. He glanced at his wristwatch. It was nearly one o'clock. It seemed like a week since he and Leroy had broken into the dock sheds.

His mother and Louise would know all about it by now. They'd phone in the morning to make sure all was well and Louise would pester him about his injections and things. She was more concerned about his diabetes sometimes than he was. It had been difficult at first, getting into the routine, but Louise had taken over from the nurse at the clinic. In the early months she ran him like a business. She made him do regular blood tests and supervised his diet. She even took the trouble to go to a chemist in Ilford who stocked American-made vitamin tablets because she discovered they had more vitamins in them. When Dad got tired of taking him to Romford Road Baths – typical of Dad that was, good at starting things but poor at sticking them out – Louise bought herself a swimming costume and came with him most Saturday mornings.

He got up and went into the bathroom. He gave himself a blood test. Everything seemed normal. He looked at himself in the bathroom mirror. A pimple had appeared on his forehead over his left eye – or was it his right eye? He always got this mirror image business wrong. He gave it a tentative squeeze but it wasn't sufficiently developed to merit the full treatment.

'I've made a cup of cocoa!' his Dad shouted from the kitchen.

Alan sauntered in. The kitchen was large and square. The sink unit was under the window and next to the electric cooker and the washing machine. He was glad to see the washing machine because last year he'd spent most mornings in the Washeteria reading comics and waiting for the spin dryer to finish the washing. Dad was very fussy about clean clothes. Even at his lowest ebb he always dressed well, trousers pressed, shirts and cufflinks, highly polished shoes and a neat tie. Alan had heard one of his mates refer to his father as a 'snappy' dresser but he wasn't sure what it meant. It seemed to please Fred though.

'Do you take sugar? Oh . . . of course you don't. Sorry,' said Connie.

She began to try to take off her leather boots. She wasn't very successful. She held her leg up to Fred who grabbed the heel and yanked the boot off. She twitched her toes; they gave the impression they were pleased to see daylight again. Fred repeated the tug-of-war on the other leg. They laughed like a couple of teenagers and then sobered up, in a slightly embarrassed fashion, when they saw Alan staring at them. He'd never got used to the idea of his Dad living with another woman. Although he'd liked the first one – Connie was number three – he felt quite guilty about it, as if he were letting his mother down by just being mildly agreeable.

Looking at Connie he realised how small she was. Sitting in the car at the school gate had given him a false notion of her size. She was about 5ft 2ins and rather plump. She was wearing a very expensive jersey suit which revealed a couple of rolls of flesh around her middle. She had slim arms and delicate hands and quite thin legs. She was a bit out of proportion now that he came to view her properly. She seemed to consist of a kind of tubby tube with thin limbs attached. Her hair was very blond although her eyebrows were dark brown. It was an attractive face made hard by too much make-up. She wasn't like any of the women he'd seen in the fashion magazines that Louise left around. She looked like somebody who was trying to give the impression she was young and with-it, and failing badly.

'Done your blood test?' his Dad asked.

'Yep. I'm OK till morning. I've brought my alarm clocks. Next injection is 7.30.'

'I hope it won't wake me up, not at 7.30,' Connie giggled. 'I'm looking forward to a lie in.'

'You'll be lucky,' muttered Dad. 'We've got a few things to do tomorrow. Oh, Alan, you can look after yourself. There's plenty in the fridge, just get what you want. If you can't be bothered cooking, the chippy's two streets away. They do a nice bit of cod, fresh cod, pearly white, isn't it Connie?'

'Yeh. It's a great chippy, Alan. We use it a lot, don't we love?' Connie scratched her armpit and yawned. 'God, I'm tired, Fred.'

'I'll take my cocoa into the bedroom . . . OK?' asked Alan.

'Yes . . . course, son. Is it warm enough?' Dad seemed pleased at his suggestion. He must have had things to talk about to Connie and Alan picked up the vibes. Taking his cocoa he returned to his room. Fred shut the door behind him. Even though the door was closed, Alan distinctly heard Connie say in a tired, resigned voice:

'Well, mastermind, how do you intend playing this one?'

And Dad replied, 'Just leave it to me, Connie. I got it all sussed out.'

Connie giggled and said something Alan couldn't catch. His Dad burst out laughing. Alan felt embarrassed. He felt like an outsider. That wasn't how Dads, good Dads, behaved.

9

A Prisoner

The alarms woke him at 7.30. Alan got up immediately and went into the bathroom. After a quick wash he administered his injections and returned to his bedroom. He dressed very quietly and then tiptoed into the kitchen and put the kettle on. It was a bright, sunny morning and from the kitchen window he could see the River Blackwater through the gap between the two bungalows at the bottom of the garden. A breeze scurried a few fluffy clouds across the blue expanse of the sky and the pleasure yachts bent their sails before it, like obedient swans. As he waited for the kettle to boil, a large yacht, much larger than the others, came into view closely followed by an old Thames sailing barge with huge brown sails. These barges were a feature of the strand at Maldon and made a pretty design of masts and sails against the tower of the church of St Mary. Sailors used its triangular tower as a navigation point. Alan could see the church from the bottom of the garden by looking to the right, across the flat marshland.

He brewed a pot of tea and buttered two rounds of toast. 'Nice day for a walk,' he muttered.

Then Alan had an idea. He put some bread in the toaster, boiled two eggs and placed them all on a tray. Breakfast for Fred and Connie, that would be a nice surprise. Balancing the tray in one hand he knocked on the bedroom door. There was no response. He knocked again. Nothing. He turned the door knob and gently opened the door. He peeped in, his face suitably furnished with a daft grin. There wasn't anybody there. It didn't look as though the bed had been slept in.

He took the tray back to the kitchen and returned to the bedroom. Standing by the bed he tried to work it out. He'd left them in the kitchen at midnight. He'd heard them moving around for half an hour or so, then . . . then he'd dropped off. There was probably a simple explanation for all this. But why had they stolen away in the night? And why not bother to have a kip? Why hadn't they said something to him? He looked around for a note. There didn't appear to be any kind of message. One of the drawers by the window was half open. Alan could see a few clean handkerchiefs, ladies underwear and . . . a syringe! Who was using a syringe? The underwear made it plain enough. The drawer was used by Connie.

'Fancy Connie being diabetic,' he thought. ''Course I don't know her very well, but . . . well, that's something we have in common.' The syringe looked a bit mucky and she didn't appear to have the rest of the kit. 'Perhaps this is just an old one she doesn't use any more,' he mused.

Alan wandered back into the kitchen. He ate the two boiled eggs and wolfed down the toast.

'No point in wasting good food,' he thought. 'Well, they did say I could look after myself. Perhaps they had it in mind even then to push off.'

Still, he didn't mind. He'd been on his own before; he could look after himself. That's what growing up was all about, his mother had said more than once. 'Learn to look after yourself, son. Never be dependent on other people, stand on your own two feet.' Well, here was a chance, just for a few days, to prove the point. He'd take a walk to Haybridge and call at the chippy on the way back. He felt in his back pocket for his wallet. It wasn't there. He ran into the bedroom and searched around the bed.

Sometimes his wallet fell out of his back pocket when he carelessly threw his jeans over a chair. He couldn't find it. Now he was in a fix. He had no money. Could it have fallen from his pocket in the car? He went over to the bedroom window which overlooked the small driveway. Both cars had gone.

'Stuck out here with no money,' he thought to himself. 'That's not much of a prospect. I need money for the chippy and a newspaper.' A newspaper, yes. That's what he wanted so that he could find out how the police were dealing with Leroy's death. But where could he get some money?

A glance at the old oak wardrobe reminded him of the hidden notes under the shoe rack. Within seconds he'd lifted the secret panel. There was no sign of the money. It had gone. He sat on the bed to think things out. This business was becoming very strange. There was something about the whole situation that didn't add up. Well, for a start he'd ring Louise.

He went out into the small hallway by the front door where the telephone was kept on a three-legged table. It wasn't there. The fixture into which it plugged was there but the cable and handset had been taken away.

Why would they take the telephone? What was going on? The situation was assuming the proportions of a nightmare. Alan returned to the kitchen and sat down.

What did it add up to? he wondered. The wallet? The money? The 'phone? Why go to the trouble? Perhaps he was exaggerating. All of these things could be explained quite easily. He could have dropped his wallet in his Dad's car. His Dad hadn't noticed and had driven away without knowing that Alan was penniless. The 'phone? Well, knowing Dad's inability to pay bills perhaps the telephone company had taken it away. As for the money in the wardrobe, well, that obviously belonged to Connie Masters and she'd taken it away to bank it. Perhaps she was a business woman. Of course, that would explain everything, and anyway she did bet on the dogs and he'd heard that lucky punters could clear a few thousand in a night at Walthamstow dog track. He'd seen somebody on TV claiming to have won five thousand on two races.

But there was still a nagging doubt. He couldn't reconcile the fact that he'd witnessed the killing of his friend and hand't been interviewed by the police. In normal circumstances he'd be spending hours at the police station 'helping the police with their enquiries' – they always said that on the news.

Why hadn't the police contacted him? Why? Then it happened. It was as if somebody had pressed a lever in his mind and his memories began to unwind in order. He'd been unable to contact the police because the man in the boiler suit had been in the hut of the security man on the dock gates. The 'phone by the pub had been broken. The tall woman with the sharp features who'd inspected the boat and the plane had entered the pub and prevented him using the 'phone there so he'd told Fred who'd said *he'd* 'phone the police. It was Fred who'd said the police didn't want to see him. It was Fred who'd suggested he come to Maldon – because the police wanted him out of the way, so Fred had said. His next question hit him so hard in the pit of his stomach that he sat down and grabbed the table for support. Supposing Fred hadn't rung the police at all? Supposing that this was one of Fred's schemes . . . ?

He closed his eyes. He didn't want to grasp the awful truth. A montage of scenes between his mother and father flicked swiftly across his memory, pictures that focused on Marcia's look of disbelief as Dad told her of his plans. There was that look of tired resignation on her face as he explained away another failure. The excuses, the lies, the unpaid bills, the demanding letters, the bluster as he lit a fag and promised everything would be all right tomorrow. Alan recalled a TV advert featuring a flash salesman. Underneath it asked 'Would you buy a car from this man?' Alan pictured his father as he winked and threw ten pound notes onto the floor. 'Could this father betray his son?' the caption said in large red letters. Alan nodded. Yes . . . he had to finally admit. Fred would exploit anybody. Fred had not rung the police. Fred was in this thing up to his neck. And Leroy was dead, murdered. Alan mused on this appalling thought but it looked just as black no matter which way you viewed it. But how could Fred make a pile out of this mess?

Alan recalled all he'd said when he'd dashed home last night. He'd told Fred every detail of his frightening experience. The information couldn't possibly be to Fred's advantage. He didn't deal in boats or light aircraft and without heavy transport nicking them was out of the question. Although the docks were empty it would still create quite a fuss and noise getting them loaded. So what was his angle? How could he milk this situation for a few quid? One thing was certain, Alan wasn't going to find out any of the answers to his questions by sitting in the kitchen. His first requirement was money. He began to search the house. People frequently leave money around the house for special purposes. A few pounds in a cup or on the shelf for the milkman or small amounts for the window cleaner and . . . Of course, he remembered. Fred always kept a 50p piece on the electricity meter box in the cellar. They'd never had the meter taken out and Fred was always sending them out to get 50p pieces in their change from the local shops.

A quick scurry down the cellar steps confirmed the

notion. As Alan flicked the light on he saw a 50p piece balanced on the top of the meter. The cellar was dusty and full of jumble. It smelt of cigarette smoke. There was a can of diesel fuel, two coils of rope, a couple of rusty lobster pots and a box of spanners. Alan recognised them as the bits and pieces that Fred used on 'Loallan'. As he gazed at the lobster pots he remembered the excitement of catching their first lobster and looking forward to having it for tea and then discovering later that Fred had flogged it to the landlord of the Block and Tackle for two crates of booze. Fred always let you down sooner or later. There were also two wooden crates in one corner, about the size of a small chest of drawers. One had been broken open and the straw had spilled out. The smell of tobacco smoke Alan had first encountered on coming down the cellar steps grew stronger as he looked into the box. At first he thought the crate was empty. Looking closer he saw just beneath a bit of straw a thin brown box. He picked it up and dusted off the straw. It was a box of cigars. Dutch cigars, or so it said on the box. 'Konigsmeinster Mild Cigars – Rolled in Holland, Half Corona.' The box was sealed. He put it back. The unopened crate contained cigars also, he assumed. He looked at the lettering burnt on the side of the crate. 'Leewarden Valcheran, Netherlands.' It seemed oddly familiar to him but he couldn't remember where he'd seen it before.

So that was Fred's latest 'scheme'. He was flogging cigars, at outrageous prices he supposed. He was probably doing a big trade in them at the dog tracks whilst Connie was betting and winning large wads, like that lot in the wardrobe.

Now that he had money he could go down to the High

Street, get a paper and 'phone Mrs Cartwright with the change.

The front door was locked, however, and the mortice locks were also in position. Alan remembered Fred always used two keys to lock up. He claimed to be frightened of burglars. Having seen the money in the wardrobe Alan now knew that Fred's fear was genuine. He tried the back door. That was double locked in the same manner. It was possible to unlock the Yale lock from inside but the mortice locks could only be unlocked with a special key. They had locked him in! He went to the kitchen window. It would be easy to climb through. It was then he noticed the locks on the windows. He examined every openable window in the house. They were all fitted with special locks. The house was burglar proof. It was also a prison.

His first inclination on discovering he was locked in was to throw a chair at a window. When he thought about it, the actual breaking of the window seemed an act of violence he was reluctant to perform. It was as if after seeing Leroy struck down he'd had the fire in his belly dowsed and put out for ever. There was still the possibility that Fred and Connie had just locked up as usual and forgotten he was asleep in the front bedroom. Very unlikely, he had to admit. After all, somebody had come into his bedroom and removed the money from beneath the hidden panel. It's true Alan's sleep was proverbially deep, hence the two alarm clocks. His Mum sometimes had to shake him awake to make sure he did his injections at the right time. Despite his conviction that they'd deliberately locked him in the house, their lack of motive for doing so still cast a shadow of doubt in Alan's mind. Suppose he knocked out a pane of glass in his bedroom just as they returned from wherever it was they'd gone? Or suppose he bashed out the window, went to get his paper, 'phoned Louise, went for a stroll and someone burgled the house through the broken window? Fred would never invite them to Maldon again. No more boat trips.

It was nearly eleven o'clock. Alan decided to make a pot of tea, have his mid-morning biscuits, perhaps check his blood sugar, and if they hadn't arrived back by that time he'd smash a window and 'phone Louise to see about getting him home – whether the police liked it or not.

A visit to the police station might be his best bet anyway. He could explain the broken window, get them to keep an eye on the place and borrow the fare to Canning Town.

An hour later Alan went down into the cellar to find a suitable weapon to smash the window. He found a rusting tool box. It contained a set of spanners that Fred used when he was messing about with his car. He selected the largest one and wrapping a tea cloth round his hand he went into his bedroom to select a window. He chose the lefthand one because there was a rose bush outside the other which could make climbing out difficult. He gave the window a tap with the spanner. It didn't break. He gave it another tap. The glass remained intact. Swinging back his arm, he gave the pane a blow which shattered it into a hundred pieces. One small piece nicked his thumb. It was whilst he was sucking it that a face appeared at the broken window. It was Louise.

'What the hell are you up to, Alan? Dad will go mad when he sees this!'

'I'm locked in. They locked me in.'

'Who locked you in?'

'Dad and Connie. All the doors and windows are locked.'

'Didn't they leave you any keys, you stupid clod?'

'I've searched all over the place. There's no sign of keys anywhere.'

'What do you intend to do now, or is that too difficult a question?'

'I'm going to climb out and now that you're here I'm going home.'

'Oh no you're not, after all the trouble you've caused. You're better out of the way for a day at least. Mum was all for coming down here and throwing you in the Blackwater.'

'All the trouble . . . what trouble are you talking about?'

'That stupid message you left in the bathroom.'

'It wasn't stupid . . . I saw it happen. I saw Leroy killed . . . murdered by two fellahs in boiler suits.'

'I 'phoned the police in a panic . . . and they came rushing round.'

'Well?'

'They'd never heard of the killing. Said they'd check.'

'Well?'

'They rang back in twenty minutes to say everything was all right. Leroy hadn't been killed and would we keep our imaginative, lying brother under lock and key for fear his lies caused some real trouble!'

'So Leroy's not dead?'

'The police say Leroy is not dead.'

'Well where is he?'

'They didn't say . . . I presume he's at home.'

Alan climbed through the window. The sunny morning and the news about Leroy raised his spirits. He didn't even mind now about breaking the window. A heavy weight of responsibility was now lifted from his mind. Perhaps now he could enjoy a day in Maldon. He'd explain the broken window to Fred and offer to pay for it out of his car cleaning money. It wouldn't cost a fortune, and anyway Fred was partly to blame for locking him in the house in the first place.

'Now what?' demanded Louise. She was peeved because she couldn't deposit her weekend case in the bedroom.

'I suppose the splashing sound I heard was Leroy diving into the dock and swimming away. He's a terrific swimmer.'

Alan smiled at his own credulity. He might have known that Leroy was only pretending to be unconscious. As soon as they put him down on the dockside he'd obviously waited till they weren't looking and dived in.

'I suppose I could push it through the window,' Louise

said crossly. She aimed the bag carefully and threw it on to Alan's bed.

'Come on, you . . . we'll go and get your fish and chips. You'll die without them. Mum has given me enough money for both of us.'

They strolled along Doris Road and turned left into the High Street. The 'Delicious Chippy' as it was called was next to the dry cleaners. Its other adjacent neighbour was John Brown and Sons, Undertakers. Louise maintained that after queuing for twenty minutes and eating the fish and chips you could choose which business to visit next – the cleaners to get the grease and smell out of your clothes or the undertakers to deal with the effects of food poisoning.

The 'Delicious Chippy' was owned by Melanie O'Reilly. She was the daughter of a big Chinese family who had a business in the Mile End Road. She'd married an Irish man from Seven Kings, Ilford, who'd died in a lorry accident leaving her with a young family. She was small, dark haired and very keen to succeed. She'd furnished the place with blue melanin-topped tables. Each table was covered with a red and white check tablecloth in the centre of which she'd placed a small pot of dried flowers supported by a glass salt cellar and a vinegar bottle. The odour of the chippy was intrusive. Alan could smell it in his pullover an hour after he'd left the place. He loved it; the clack and clang of the lids on the fryers as Melanie banged them shut after manoeuvring the chips around the hot orange-brown fat. Its bubbling attack on the bare white chips was music that made his taste buds tingle. Melanie sang Irish ballads all the time she was cooking and for no obvious reason raised her voice to operatic proportions as she dipped the fish into a trough of yellow batter and slid them into the fat. It reminded

Alan of a film he'd seen of piranha fish attacking a body in the Amazon as the fat bubbled and sizzled around the fishy flesh. Today she was singing 'The Mountains of Mourne' in her cockney accent.

'. . . so I just took a hand in this digging for gold . . . but for all that I found there I might as well be where the Mountains of Mourne sweep down to the sea.' The word 'sea' was sung on a prolonged and warbling note as she banged down the cover over the frying fat, opened the chip fryer, gave the chips a stir, banged it shut again and turned to smile at Alan and Louise.

'Now, you two . . . visiting your Dad? Brought the nice weather with you. What you like?'

'Cod and chips twice,' Alan said quickly, eager to get down to the eating business. He didn't want any discussion with Louise who always stood there wondering whether she should widen her fish experience by trying skate or rock salmon or whether she should have roast chicken instead. She didn't appear to be in a mood for considering her more mature attitudes to food, so she sat down at a table and undid her shoulder bag. She examined her face in a hand mirror.

'You've got a spot on your chin,' Alan said helpfully. She gave him a fierce look and then quickly checked the statement.

'It's only a redness . . . it's not an actual spot.'

'Could develop,' Alan said. 'They usually do with you.'

'It's going to be one of those days, is it?'

'What days?'

'Days when you provoke me into a temper.'

'No.' He looked around to see if Melanie had got the chips sorted out.

'In the light of your recent behaviour you'd better be nice to me so that I can square our Mum and prevent her from doing you serious damage. She nearly had a heart attack when I showed her your message and she went puce when she discovered you'd gone off with Dad . . . and what was he doing in the flat anyway? Mum didn't realise he had a key.'

'I didn't realise he had a key either,' said Alan, still looking towards Melanie. 'He was just sat there when I arrived. I was so upset I didn't think to wonder why he was there. I presumed he was going to meet Mum.'

'He's up to something . . . God, haven't we had enough without him starting his trouble again.' Louise replaced her mirror in the bag and closed it.

'He's doing something . . . some kind of business with cigars.'

'Cigars? How do you know?'

'He's got a couple of crates in the basement . . . Dutch cigars.'

'What does he know about cigars?'

'How should I know? You know him. He's a trader. He'll flog anything . . . anything that makes a few bob.'

'Money melts in his hands like hot butter.'

'Well, he's got a bit stacked away at the moment.'

'How do you know?'

'I saw it . . . about £2,000 I'd say, in the wardrobe . . . but it's gone now.'

'Another of your bloody lies. Why do you do it? Tell lies?'

'I don't. It's the truth. Everything I've told you is the truth. That note was the truth . . . well, the truth as I saw it. I don't tell lies about big things. I thought they'd killed Leroy . . . and so would you if you'd been there.'

'You shouldn't have been there and then all this wouldn't have happened. That den place you two go to is out of bounds . . . they could take you to court for trespass. Now, come on, Alan. I want the truth. What did happen?'

Heaving a sigh Alan told her everything he'd seen in the shed on Friday night. Louise asked him a question or two and as his story unfolded, she became very interested.

Melanie shouted, 'Alan!' She never forgot a name. 'Alan, cod and chips twice!'

Louise gave him a five pound note. Jumping up quickly he went to the counter and collected two plates of fish and chips. Alan pushed some of his chips onto Louise's plate. Too many chips would raise his blood sugar. He placed the food on the table before his sister. She looked at his plate and then her own. She smiled. She couldn't help enjoying Alan's necessary sacrifices, particularly when she benefited from them.

'Too many fatty chips could make you bulge in all the wrong places,' he said without looking up. He knew she savoured his discomfort on these occasions. He dissected the fried fish cleanly and removed the batter. Batter isn't good for diabetics either.

When he'd eaten the fish he winkled out a gherkin from a jar on the table and crammed it into his mouth. He sucked it noisily. Louise considered him a disgusting eater. As he crunched the last tasty shreds of the pickle he looked forward to messing about in his Dad's boat, 'Loallan'. The boat was a reminder of his Dad's better nature. His experiences on the river were pleasant to recall.

Alan forked a couple of chips. He was about to eat them when the door opened and the lady in the white mac came in followed by the tall, well-built man in rubber boots he'd seen in the shed.

He put the chips back on his plate. He'd lost his appetite.

10

In the Net

Alan reached across the table and tapped Louise's arm.
'What?'
'That woman,' he nodded towards her back as she ordered a 'take away' at the counter. 'Don't turn round. The woman I saw in Shed 22 is there.'

Louise glanced round casually. She nodded.

'Who is she with? Is he part of your story too?'

'Yes . . . he was with her and he's a friend of Connie's too.' Alan took a good look at the man from behind the protection of the menu to make sure. He wore an oilskin and a blue peaked cap. He looked like the same sailing man, a man who earned a living from boats. His hands were calloused and stained with work. He certainly wasn't an office type. He spoke to the woman in the mac in a foreign language. She replied in the same tongue. Louise took a second longer look at the woman. Melanie placed her food in two boxes and wrapped them in newspaper. As she passed them over the counter she said something to the man which made him smile and nod. Turning, the woman and the sailor left.

'She's worth a lot of money. Her clothes are fabulous. That mac and those shoes cost a fortune.'

Alan got up and went to the window to see which way they went. He caught a glimpse of them making their way down to the quays before they were lost in the bustle of holiday-makers. He sat down again at the table. Louise was just finishing her meal. She wiped her mouth with a white serviette.

'That's the demon woman then. She looks quite average to me, except for the clothes, of course. She's rich, that's for sure.'

Alan had an idea.

'Do you want a cup of tea?'

''Course . . . but no sugar for you, remember.'

Alan went to the counter.

'Two teas, please, Melanie, and do you mind me asking . . . who were those people who bought the take aways just now?'

'Don't know her at all . . . never been here before . . . but the fellah is a boat owner. Comes here often from Holland. He lives in Rotterdam, he told me once. His boat's a big green one. I think it's called "Tregammon". He bought it here a year ago. I saw him painting it last November. Keeps it in the shed next to Murchison and Drew . . . you know, on the opposite quay to the yard where your Dad keeps his new boat?'

A customer entered and Melanie served her. Alan returned to the table.

'Melanie says the man is Dutch and he has a boat . . . a boat called "Tregammon". That's the boat I saw in Shed 22. And another thing. Melanie says Dad has got a *new* boat! Did you know he'd got a new boat? What's happened to "Loallan"?'

'A new boat? She must be mistaken. He couldn't afford a new suit, or so he told our Mum. A new boat? Well, let's go and have a look.'

They walked quickly up the High Street and turned down the sloping Quay Road that curved round onto the quayside of the River Blackwater. Maldon was an ancient seafaring town whose history went back in time to those days when the sea was the main means of communication between places of importance. It had even been the site of a Viking battle and was, and is, a town with strong seatrading connections. Sailing barges, still to be seen, used to carry corn to London till the early part of this century. The boat building shed of Murchison and Drew was a local landmark on the quayside. Its tall wooden structure, taller than anything else around it, made it possible to house and build the larger type of inshore fishing vessel. Vessels of this kind were still in demand and fished regularly in the North Sea. Alan had seen a new one being built every year they'd been to Maldon. There was always one being fitted out, moored to the quayside whilst another was in the shed being built.

Walking quickly to Dobbin Road Quay they could see a fishing vessel moored amongst the barges. At a glance the green one resembled 'Tregammon', but Alan and Louise were more interested in finding their father's new boat. The little shed at Dobbin Road Quay where 'Loallan' was kept wasn't locked. The door was partly opened. They went inside. 'Loallan' was there in the centre of the shed and raised on wooden blocks. There was a heavy smell of fresh paint. Despite the dimness of the shed they could see that their small fishing dinghy was a dull grey. Somebody was giving her an undercoat before painting and repairing her for the summer trade, when Dad hired her out to groups of sea anglers. A young lad with blond hair of about eighteen was slapping the paint on the little cabin that covered the bow. It was the fellow Alan had seen greasing the slipway in Shed 22.

'Who are you? You're not allowed in here!' he said. He cast a worried look around. He needed some support against the intruders.

'I'm Louise and that's my father's boat you're painting.'

He smiled. 'Oh, well . . . sorry . . . that's all right come in. Mr Hogan will be along shortly . . . but I suppose you know that already. I'll just get on with this painting if you don't mind. I've got to finish it by 5 o'clock and it's nearly 3 o'clock already.'

'Where's Dad's new boat?' Alan asked, trying to be quite casual about it.

'It's tied up alongside.' The lad pointed with his paint brush to the quay which ran outside the open-ended shed.

Alan and his sister walked over to the quay, and there it was, a small ketch, painted blue and white, bobbing and glinting on the tide. It was about 40 ft long with a covered cockpit and a small gangway leading from shore to deck. In gold letters on the prow it read 'Shangri La'.

'The cigar business must pay good money!' exclaimed Louise.

'It's secondhand, it's not new,' Alan said with a touch of disappointment in his voice.

'It's thirty or forty thousand pounds worth of boat,' Louise said. 'Now where could he have got that kind of cash?'

'Could be on hp.' Alan offered.

'Would you trust our Dad on hp?' she exclaimed.

'Well, come on. If it belongs to Dad we can have a look at it I suppose.' Louise stopped halfway across the gangplank. 'Come on, Alan. You're not scared, are you?'

'I think we ought to wait till Dad comes . . . then he can show us round . . . perhaps take us out into the river?'

Alan noticed that there was some kind of movement in one of the four portholes beneath the deck-house. He bent down on the quayside to get a better view. He could see into the cabin beneath the cockpit. Connie Masters was sitting there on a kind of bunk bed. She was injecting herself with a syringe.

'Oh, so I was right,' he thought to himself. 'She *is* diabetic.'

He joined Louise on the gangplank.

'Connie Masters is down below,' he said. 'You haven't met her, have you? She's quite . . . attractive.' Louise hesitated. She really wasn't ready at that moment to meet Dad's latest girlfriend. She had great difficulty in coming to terms with her father. She found his taste in women another reason for regarding him as a no-hoper, a failure, and incurable loser. All his 'lady friends' took him for a ride. They flattered him, spent his money and left. Connie had obviously boarded him on a high tide in his affairs and no doubt she would desert him when he was knee deep in Maldon mud.

Louise walked off the gangplank and turned to Alan.

'I'm going to do some shopping. I'll meet you by "Loallan" in an hour. OK?'

'Oh . . . yes . . . right . . . see you later then.'

He watched her disappear through the shed. The blond lad gave her a wink which she ignored.

Connie stuck her head out of the cockpit and shouted, 'Who the hell are you and what are you doing on this boat?'

Alan raised a hand to attract Connie's attention.

'It's Alan. Is Dad anywhere about?' Alan smiled.

Connie seemed to have difficulty focusing her eyes. It was a full two seconds before she realised who it was.

'She must be quite shortsighted,' he thought.

'Oh . . . it's you . . . Alan . . . well . . . well now . . . what can I do for you?'

'I thought you could let me have a look around the boat,' Alan said rather pointedly. 'Is Dad about?'

'Well, no . . . he won't be long. The boat's very untidy at the moment and I've got to use the 'phone in a few minutes. Look, why don't you just sit here in the cockpit whilst I tidy up in the cabin and when I've made my call we'll have a cup of tea . . . or something. How about that?'

'OK,' said Alan. 'Sorry if I've caught you at a bad moment.' He noticed that Connie in retreating into the cabin held on to the rail to steady herself. 'Has she been drinking?' he wondered. 'She looks pissed to me. Still, that's what all his girlfriends are like . . . cheap and boozy. I'll sit by the wheel and wait. Dad won't be long.'

As he watched the river traffic and enjoyed the afternoon sun he could hear Connie tidying up below and things falling to the floor. Drawers were shut and dishes were flung noisily into the sink. After about ten minutes Connie emerged. She was wearing a blue and white striped sweater, jeans, a black yachting cap and an enormous pair of dark sunglasses. She smiled in a strained kind of way.

'Well, that's tidied things up a bit. I've put the kettle on. I'll just go and make this 'phone call. The biscuits are in the round red tin on the top shelf,' she called as she wobbled unsteadily across the gangplank.

Alan climbed down into the cabin. It was quite spacious. The dining table occupied the middle of the area and the bunks were converted into upholstered seating. In the far righthand corner were a sink unit and cooker. Apart from the portholes the walls were taken up with polished softwood cupboards. It all looked very expensive. The forward cabin was quite narrow and it accommodated two bunk beds and a toilet. The cabins smelt of mansion polish and a faint whiff of cigars.

'If he's making this much money out of cigars,' Alan thought, 'I mustn't be surprised if he smokes one or two himself.' Alan poured tea into a red enamel mug and added milk from a bottle in the little fridge by the sink.

He sat and sipped his tea and gazed around. The smell

of tobacco was quite odd. He'd had this sensation somewhere before. Within seconds he remembered a party in Poplar. It had been a really boring do until the parents went to the pub. Two lads produced this stuff, cannabis, and they'd all had a go at it. The smell in the cabin was just like the whiff the parents had got when they came back from the pub and chucked everybody out in the street. It was two years ago now, but there was no mistaking the smell. Connie, he decided, wasn't drunk, she was high.

Alan washed and wiped the mug and put it in a cupboard above the sink. A stub of a cigar nestled in an ashtray wedged behind the taps. He picked it out and was about to throw it into the waste bucket when he heard a sound behind him.

'Can't manage till tea-time, eh?'

Alan looked round. The young painter was leaning down into the cabin, looking and smiling at him.

'Just helping yourself, eh! Well, I suppose that's all right if you're the boss's son.'

'What?'

'I've come for a few perks . . . you know . . . he lets me have a few as part of me wages. I can get a good bit for them round here at weekends.' He pointed to the cigar stub in Alan's hand. 'There's quite a trade when there's a good gig around and plenty of people coming in to Maldon to enjoy themselves. You could make a hundred quid on a good night. Could you pass me the tin from the cupboard?'

He pointed to the cupboard above the sink. Alan reached up and opened it.

'It's the long orange box,' he said.

Alan recognised the box as being identical to the one

that had contained the money in the wardrobe. He passed it across to the painter.

'Been on it a while, have you? Bit young for the hard stuff, aren't you? 'Course, I don't touch it myself.' He undid the metal clips and took out several small plastic packets. He put three or four in his jacket pocket closed the box and handed it back.

'Oh, don't say anything to Connie. She's not keen on me having a little stake in the business but your Dad's OK. He's a real sport, he don't mind sharing the goodies. After all, he's making a pile. Lovely idea them cigars. Very clever. Well, cheers, mate. It's off for me. Taking a bird to Southend. Could get rid of a bit there, I reckon. Regards to your Dad. Cheers. Oh yeh, and whilst I remember, tell him Alec is available for crewing next Thursday and Friday. I'll sort out the tides and give him a tinkle. OK?'

When Alan was sure that Alec was clear of the quayside he reached up and pulled out three more orange containers. Each had an identical hook moulded into the thick endpiece. He opened the boxes. Two contained packets of the white powder. The other two were packed tight with used bank notes. He put them back and began searching for cigars. He pulled out two or three drawers but they only contained clothes, mostly shirts and waterproofs. He climbed into the cockpit. A green jacket was draped over the seat behind the wheel. Feeling guilty, he searched the pockets. In the breast pocket he found a cigar. He looked at it and smelt it. It was just a cigar as far as he could see. He took it down into the cabin and placed it on the side of the sink. Finding a sharp knife in the drawer he cut the cigar in two lengthways. He fully expected to find ten pound notes folded inside. What he found was a thin transparent tube of white powder surrounded by a fibrous weedy substance. The tobacco leaves were a cleverly constructed container for drugs.

'Now you know everything, I wonder what we must do with you.'

The voice from behind was icy clear and spiced with a foreign accent.

Turning, Alan found himself facing the woman in the white mac, her Dutch seaman friend and Connie. The woman was pointing a polished silver pistol straight at his heart.

11

The Pick Up

They tied Alan's hands together and bundled him into the forward cabin. He could make out most of what they had to say when they spoke in English.

He hadn't spoken a word since their arrival. He'd read in adventure stories how people in these circumstances always managed to say the right things just at the appropriate moment. Alan didn't utter a single syllable. The impact and shock of his discovery of a drug ring in which is father was an important link left him speechless. He also realised how little he knew about his captors. Again, he remembered how in books every character was laid out before the reader in great detail. Vivid descriptions of their looks, meaningful smiles, sardonic grins, bulging eyes etc., etc. In the past twenty-four hours he had seen two men in boiler suits, one of whom he'd later seen on the bus, a woman in a white mac and her sailor friend who lived in Rotterdam, a painter named Alec, and Connie. Connie and Alec were known to him by name but the others were complete strangers. This was obviously how it happened in real life, a hectic blur of impressions, no clear details. That's what the police sometimes complained about when taking statements from witnesses. People didn't really see very much. Their eyes are often turned within themselves, not constantly searching, quizzing and storing detailed information to be repeated in a court of law. That's how it really was. Perhaps whilst he was awaiting his fate he'd better commit some information to memory in case he got the chance to tell the police.

The woman in the white mac was obviously number one in the organisation. She dominated the other two. Her voice was the one he heard raised highest in the argument that raged when they locked him away. Connie was told in no uncertain terms that she was an incompetent junkie and that after this operation she was to disappear. As the woman put it, 'Your taste for the high life is not matched by a competency of sufficient calibre to achieve it.'

The Dutchman barely spoke except to say in broken English that, 'De boy is a big problem to our operation tonight. We must be rid of him.'

Odd, thought Alan, how a total stranger that you've never spoken to can suddenly decide to terminate your existence. Connie got upset about this and said murder wasn't part of the bargain but when asked what else she could suggest she went dumb. After another half hour's talk, Alan heard the boat's engine start into life. A few minutes later it was moving slowly out into mid-stream. It was like leaving the safety of home. As long as the boat was attached to the quayside there was always a chance, but now that they were on their way who could help him? His one hope was Louise. She'd come back and see the woman in the white mac and take action. Louise wasn't stupid. She was out there somewhere telling somebody and sorting out the whole sorry mess. And then he fell asleep.

He woke up as a hand gently shook his shoulder.

'Hallo, Alan,' his Dad said. 'Are you all right? Glad you got a bit of a sleep. They didn't hurt you did they?'

Alan started to cry so his Dad nursed him.

'Can you untie the rope round my wrists, Dad?'

Fred shook his head sadly. He indicated the others beyond the door and then touched his lips with his forefinger. 'I can't do anything until I've sorted out a way to get you off this boat. You really have ballsed it up for me. Don't get worried, it wasn't your fault. I thought if I locked you in the bungalow you'd just watch the telly and feed yourself till I got back.'

'I smashed a window.'

'Well, that wasn't the brightest thing to do in the circumstances.' Fred got up and had a peep at the others through the half open door. He came back.

'Look . . . son. When you dashed in last night and told me you'd been at Shed 22 I could have died. I've been working on my scheme . . . and it's a big scheme, son . . . with Margarite and Sven for months now. It's a real money spinner. Another month or two and it's a villa in Spain. You, Louise and your mother out there in the sun all day, wanting for nothing . . . cars . . . trips . . . a yacht . . . the lot.'

'But Dad. You always lose. You'll get caught. You know you will.'

'It's foolproof, son. Absolutely foolproof. Well it was . . . '

'Was?'

'Till you turned up. They'll not tolerate a lad of thirteen being in the know. They want you out of it . . . for good.

'But you won't let them, Dad? They won't kill me. You wouldn't let 'em do that for all the money . . . would you?'

' 'Course not, son . . . trust me.'

'Where are we?'

'We're docked near "Tregammon" on the quay opposite Dobbin Road. We just tested the engines downstream a bit then returned and tied up. The full tide is in two hours so we'll be mobile in about an hour's time. You just keep quiet and out of sight. In all the excitement they might just forget about you . . . and that's your best shot, OK?'

Alan nodded. Again he was conscious of his inability to respond like kids do on the TV with phrases like, 'Don't worry, Dad. We'll see this thing through,' or, 'No matter what, Dad, I'll always love you as my father,' etc. But nothing came to mind, so he nodded, and as a last minute gesture he winked. This took his Dad by surprise but he nodded and smiled back. Alan heard the bolt on the door clang as it was thrust across.

He sat up and after a struggle managed to move so that he could see through the porthole. The quayside was lit up and several boats were obviously preparing to sail on the same tide. The fishing boat immediately ahead of them was very busy as three men loaded box after box on board, using a small motorised truck. Alan presumed the boxes were for the catch. He'd seen them landing the fish sometimes. They'd sort them out and ice them over in the boxes ready to be auctioned at the quayside for the big London fish market. As he watched, one of the men in a boiler suit looked up into the dock lights and then straight at Alan. He recognised him immediately. It was one of the men in the boiler suits who'd caught Leroy. The man saw him. He grinned. He seemed to be saying OK and he put his thumbs up. He's obviously talking to someone on deck, Alan decided. They were all in it together, that was obvious. Tonight was a big night and they were all going to be taking part.

The 'Shangri La' got under way and manoeuvred its way into the Blackwater River. Alan saw a couple of navigation lights and the distant light of a house on land.

He heard the occasional footstep above him on the deck and the steady throb of the engine. His Dad came to see him for a few minutes.

'OK, son?' he asked.

Alan just looked at him. 'OK, Dad.'

'Won't be long now. Another twenty minutes.'

'How are you going to get me off this boat?'

His Dad tapped his nose and smiled. 'It's a secret, son . . . you'll see!' and he was gone again.

Alan searched the sea for other craft but it was pitch black. If you wanted to get rid of somebody by throwing them overboard this was the time and place to do it. The engines slowed. After a few minutes they stopped. Footsteps overhead multiplied. A small searchlight suddenly stabbed the darkness on the port side. Looking out Alan couldn't see anything at first. The beam slowly scanned the waves. The light was switched off. There was an angry conversation on deck. The light was switched on again. The pencil of light fingered the darkness. What was it looking for? Then into the beam sprang a row of orange lights. Alan counted twelve of them. There was a whoop of delight on deck. The engine started up and slowly the boat edged its way towards the orange markers. Someone reached over the side with a hooked pole and pulled up one of the orange markers. It was another of the orange cannisters he'd seen in the wardrobe at the bungalow. The 'Shangri La' collected them all. The searchlight was switched off and the boat turned in the direction of Maldon. Alan heard voices in the next cabin. He sat by the locked door and strained to hear what was being said.

He could make out Margarite saying that she'd been a bit worried that her calculations had not been accurate.

'I've practised dropping them from a plane for months

in Holland,' she said. 'British tides are so unpredictable.'
She laughed. 'Where did you get the idea of the chemical
rope, Fred?'

'I saw it on an old black and white film one Sunday
afternoon. This actor called William Powell was on the
trail of drug runners and they dumped the stuff overboard
in containers with weights so they sank to the bottom.
After the sea water reacted with the chemicals at the
weighted end of the rope they just bobbed up when the
police weren't looking and the baddies came and
collected. It was easy. Dropping the stuff from a plane is
our idea. And it works.'

They all laughed and had a few drinks. Alan was
beginning to think they'd forgotten about him when he
heard the Dutchman speak.

'De problem of de boy . . . we cannot risk his mouth.
He may promise you, but others, less gentle would wring
it out of him.'

'I've sorted it all out, to all our satisfaction. He's a
diabetic . . . know what that is, do ye?'

'Of course. We have many diabetics in Holland.'

'Well, if he don't have his injection he goes into a coma
and he dies in a kind of sleep if he isn't seen to. So . . . he
hasn't got his kit with him in there . . . '

'Very neat,' said Margarite. 'Tomorrow you discover
him dead in the boat . . ., an unfortunate accident.'

'Oh no. Better than that,' interrupted Fred. 'We carry
him into a quiet place behind one of the harbour buildings
and leave him there. That way it's nothing to do with
boats, just an unfortunate boy who's died of diabetes.
Very clever, no bruises, no bullets, no bangs on the
head . . .'

'I think we ought to make sure,' the sailor said.

'Don't be stupid,' said Margarite. 'We've another month of this yet.'

Alan came away from the door. He sat on the bunk. What his Dad had told the gang wasn't true. If he went without his glucose tablets or his insulin he'd go into a series of hypos but he wouldn't die. Dying only resulted from continuous neglect. Might take three or four days. He'd be extremely ill, but he wouldn't die. He was sure Dad knew this . . . or did he? Did he really think he'd die? One thing was certain, if Margarite accepted Dad's story he'd survive till they got back to Maldon. Then what?

Things went quiet in the cabin. After about ten minutes the door opened and Connie came in.

'Where are you, Alan?' she called. There was no light in the cabin.

'I'm here,' he said miserably.

She came over and placed something on his lap. Before he could respond she'd gone and locked the door behind her. Feeling with his fingers he soon recognised the object as his own tube of glucose tablets. They'd removed them when he'd been tied up. Connie hadn't noticed that his hands were still tied. He manoeuvred the tube into the crease between the seat and the back support of the upholstery. Working with his fingers, he undid the screw top and tipped the tube so that most of the tablets fell out onto the seat. Turning round and kneeling he chased the tablets across the seat till he could get them near his mouth.

He was about to take one into his mouth when a thought struck him. Supposing he didn't take any glucose? He'd soon have a hypo. If he could risk going into a coma they'd think he was dying. Dad could then persuade them to leave him in a dark place and arrange for him to be found. Yes! It was worth the risk. He pushed the tablets away. He'd trust his Dad just once more.

The engines stopped again. After a few minutes' silence he heard the splash of oars. From the porthole he saw a two-man canoe emerge from the darkness. Two men in wet suits manoeuvred the canoe alongside. The orange boxes had been strapped in twos. The canoeists draped them across the structure so that the boxes hung on either side. They then pushed off and disappeared into the darkness.

Without warning the darkness disappeared in a blaze of white light. The 'Shangri La' was fully illuminated on port and starboard. Connie screamed. A megaphone voice called, 'This is Her Majesty's Custom Officers. Heave to! You are under arrest.'

It was all rather confusing after that. Alan heard a couple of shots and then silence. He heard Connie whimpering. Two boats came alongside and men in boiler suits jumped aboard. The door to his cabin opened and somebody shone a powerful torch on him.

'Come on out, son. You're safe. Everything's OK.'

Looking up he could make out the features of the man in the boiler suit who'd given him the thumbs up sign.

'It's OK lad. I'm the police,' he said grinning.

On deck the police were arresting the Dutchman and Margarite. Connie was kneeling on the deck next to Fred who was stretched out and bleeding.

Alan ran and knelt down beside him.

'Are you all right, Dad?' He couldn't think what else to say.

'It was an accident, son. She had the best of intentions. She's not very good with a gun. She panicked a bit. I'll be all right, don't worry. I fooled 'em, son . . . about the fainting. They didn't understand.'

'I know, Dad. It worked just as you said.'

'Told you, lad. Trust your Dad. I've never let you down.'

He reached up and pulled Alan down so that he could whisper in his ear. 'There's something for you in shoe box in the wardrobe.' He creased his pale cheek into a quick wink. Alan grasped his hand but Fred was looking at Connie and patting her hand.

'I don't want the rotten money,' Alan wanted to shout, but he didn't. As he watched, Connie lit a fag and gave it to him. Fred reached forward to take a drag. Then he slumped forward. He was dead.

Alan was whipped away by the police. When he got to the quayside, Marcia and Louise were there. His hypo was now well on its way. He began to lose his temper. Instead of running to his mother he stood and pointed a finger at her.

'It's all your fault . . . the orange boxes . . . the boxes are the wrong colour for 'Shangri La' . . . and Louise, you should have . . . you should have . . . and . . . and I'm fed up with you all . . . and that's final . . . so . . .'

He passed out and was taken to a waiting ambulance where a doctor was standing by. He gave him a glucose drip in his arm and after ten minutes Alan was sitting side by side with Louise and his mother. They'd heard about Fred. They were trying to absorb the information just as his system was absorbing the sugar. It would be tomorrow before the truth sank in.

All Louise said was, 'He couldn't even die properly. He had to die by accident.'

The ambulance man came to close the doors.

'Just move up, will you. I've got another passenger.'
Leroy got in and sat opposite Alan. He grinned.

'Thought I'd come and surprise you.' Alan grasped his hand. Marcia put her arms around both their shoulders.

'Leroy,' she said, 'You're a nice lad but if you ever take Alan near those bloody sheds again I'll kill you myself.'

The ambulance started up. After a check-up at the hospital, they were taken to a hotel in Maldon for the night.

As the sun streamed through the curtains of the hotel bedroom, Alan turned over in bed to gaze into the early morning sky. His first feeling was one of relief: the boat journey and the death of his father seemed a nightmare from which he'd just woken. But then the strangeness of the room, the unfamiliar wallpaper, the wash basin and mirror by the built-in wardrobe all destroyed the illusion. A dumb, incomprehensible sadness spread over him. He lay there deliberately avoiding a replay of the events of the previous evening. The memory of his father, however, was insistent. Alan pictured him smiling, fishing rod in hand and pointing to a bank of reeds. 'There's a pike in there, Alan . . . just tease him out.' Alan turned and buried his head in the pillow. He beat the bed in an attempt to drive the image away.

'I'll never see him again . . . ever!' The full horror of the thought echoed round his mind.

It was some time before his thoughts turned to his mother. A wave of anxiety swept through his body. 'I'm responsible for Mum and Louise now,' he thought, 'and it's all your fault. You didn't have to die.' He burrowed deeper into the pillow and wept.

The next morning Leroy sat at breakfast in the dining room. He hated runny eggs and had insisted on his being hardboiled. Alan watched him carefully peel the shell and swallow the egg in two bites.

'Well?' Alan said impatiently.

'Well what?' Leroy tidied the wreckage of the splintered shell into a neat pile in the middle of his plate.

'What happened at the shed when they jumped you and carried you off?'

'They were a bit rough on me. They thought I was a drug smuggler. I could have been armed. I picked up a rusty metal bar to defend myself. One of them took it off me and threw a punch. I was out like a light. I came to briefly as they bundled me into the van and then I heard one of them on his radio asking for instructions. I thought they were going to kill me. I picked up a sledge hammer that they carry in their vans for breaking down doors on raids. It missed and fell in the dock. Then I passed out again.'

'So the splash was the sledge hammer?'

'Did you hear it?'

'I thought it was you being got rid of like that fellah that was strangled and dumped two weeks ago.'

'Well it wasn't.' Leroy grinned. 'So you thought I was a goner?'

'I've never been so frightened,' Alan said shaking his head. 'And to think we would have bungled the entire police operation.'

Leroy reached across the table and grabbing the jug of fruit juice emptied it into his glass.

'When I came to in the police station there was a hell of a row. The chap in charge of the stake-out was shouting at everybody and blaming the Sergeant for us being on the premises.

'"A stake-out on a major crime," he screamed, "and you let a slip of a kid through. How do I know the place isn't full of kids from Canning Town Youth Club playing hide and seek?" He was so angry I waited until he'd gone before I told them about you. Then my mother turned up with Ellery Johnson. Ellery was really upset by the state of my face and was about to take on a bit of the action but the Superintendent came in and explained what we'd done and how we nearly spoiled everything.'

'What happened then?'

'Well, me mother turns round to me and gives me a punch on the other side of me face. She did more damage than the police. She knocked a tooth out.' Leroy opened his mouth to reveal the gap. It had a piece of egg wedged in it. 'They took me to hospital where I was X-rayed and everything. The excitement brought on a bit of me asthma so they kept me in. It was very convenient for the police and I was in no hurry to go home after the way me mother had behaved.'

'I've got that to come I suppose. Mum hasn't said much up till now.'

'You might get away with it. Diabetes seems to generate more sympathy! When your mother told the police they nearly called off the stake-out in the river. They thought you might die if you didn't have your injections. But Louise was certain you had your kit with you so they took a chance.'

'Louise will have a go at me for sure,' Alan muttered.

'I've an idea that'll get you out of it all,' Leroy said casually.

'Oh, what's that?'

'Well if you look through the window into the High Street you'll see a sign over the Parish Hall advertising Miss Goodthorpe's Academy of Dance. Nip over there for a few quick lessons and surprise your mother with your secret talent. Whip off one of these tablecloths and do a Gene Kelly . . . in French. She'll be speechless.'

Alan would have been tempted into a smile but his mother came in with Louise and he spent the rest of breakfast trying not to cry.

12

Aftermath

Two alarm clocks shattered Alan's dream. As he scrubbed the back of his head in irritation he recalled fleetingly the image of Miss Twist, his form teacher, climbing into the navigation seat of his BMW rally car. She was kitted out with overalls and helmet. As he put the car into gear she began shouting out directions for the start of the International Docklands Rally.

He smiled. Even within the fantasy of the dream he'd been astonished at Miss Twist's sudden appearance, just as surprised as he had been by her kindness and understanding twelve months ago on his return to school after his father's death at Maldon. In those first difficult weeks a new Miss Twist had emerged. She'd raged at the press who'd attempted to interview him at school, and, with the help of the teachers of the PE department, she made sure he wasn't harassed in school again. She visited Marcia and Louise during that limbo time when neighbours and friends waited for the facts to emerge before committing themselves to visiting or to offering their condolences. She had also visited him in hospital after finding him having a hypo in the stock room.

Seeing a picture of your father in the press under headlines like 'Drug Baron Dead', 'Drug-Running Scum Pay The Price' was a humiliating experience. Bill Walker from Class 4m called him 'a pusher's scum-bag'. Bill was just out of his second probationary year for car theft. A girl from the Lower Sixth who had only recently come to Westmoreland Road School, kicked him in the dining hall and also in the street on his way home. He managed to keep himself together until the night he came home and discovered that somebody at school had placed a pile of dog-dirt in his satchel. He broke his diet, ate whatever he wanted, didn't inject himself and stopped doing his blood tests. Louise and Marcia were too busy dealing with their own problems to notice. That's when Miss Twist found him in the stock room.

'We can't be responsible for delinquent parents,' she said on one of her visits to the hospital. 'Parents are supposed to know better.' Louise was there too. It was after a chat with her on the way home that Louise applied to a large teaching hospital in London. After working and studying there for two months she seemed to have found the job she was looking for.

It was Miss Twist who supported Alan throughout the court case. He was a prime witness. Despite his nervousness he answered the questions as truthfully as he could in a quiet, clear voice. On the second day of the trial, when giving evidence against the Dutch seaman, he told the court of his father's lie about the effects of diabetes and how it had stopped the Dutchman throwing him overboard. That had been Miss Twist's idea too. 'Drug Trafficker Saves Son' was a headline in which he found a little comfort.

After the trial, Gary proved very helpful and supportive. He punched two Italian reporters and threw a French photographer out of their flat. He also arranged for a 'minder' to make sure they were 'looked after'. As Gary explained at the time, 'It's like this, Marcia. Your Fred and his cigar business is a good story. It's worth a bomb to foreign newspapers. A photograph of you and the kids could be worth a couple of grand if it was syndicated round the world. This story will appear in

Australia and Japan and all over the place. Now, if you want me to be your agent in this matter I could guarantee you a few thou . . . '

'Just stop 'em getting in the flat, Gary. I don't want to make a cent out of this dirty mess.'

Gary arranged Dad's funeral. It was all done very quickly and in secrecy. He hired the hearse from a friend and provided a couple of cars from the garage forecourt. There were only nine people at the Crematorium: Marcia, Alan, Louise, Gary, Mrs Cartwright from upstairs, Miss Twist and the Headmaster, Mr McDonald, and two Detectives from the Drug Squad. The Vicar was kind and suggested that Fred's last act in saving Alan's life would be taken into account at the 'final reckoning' and reminded those present that 'all sinners, so who shall cast the first stone'. Alan put his arm round his Mum as she shook in grief. Louise stared stonily ahead, determined not to cry.

Alan stretched, yawned and got out of bed. As he dried his face in the bathroom he saw the jammed traffic on Canning Town flyover. A line of nappies flagged the message that the young mother opposite had produced another baby. He could see the near-completed Stolport; the first flights to Amsterdam and Paris were to commence in a few weeks' time.

In the kitchen he put two eggs in a pan and turned the hotplate on. Only two eggs were required now that Louise lived at the hospital. Placing two pieces of bread in the toaster he sat down to wait. He began to think about the essay he'd written for his English homework. Miss Twist had asked the class to write about a personal experience that had made a deep impression on them. Alan had a quiet word with her after school a couple of days ago to ask if it was appropriate for him to write about his adventure. She explained that writing the story might offend his Mum but if he could recall of some of the thoughts that had passed through his mind at the time it might make a nice piece of work for his folder.

'I wonder if anyone has noticed,' he wrote, 'that when the bad guys get shot in TV series we are pleased that they've copped it? The telly never shows them being buried. You never know if they have a wife and kids or a mother who loves them. The hero gets the girl and lives happily ever after and the bad guys are forgotten. The actors who play these parts are called "bit part" players. They're there to keep the story going. That's all. What happens to those James Bond women? Do they have parents who cry at their funeral?'

Once he'd got started on the subject he couldn't stop writing. Without revealing too much detail, he described how those weeks had been full of unpleasant events that had appeared like a boil on his back unannounced. It had been a a painful interlude, but now, in quieter times, the skin of his life had grown over the painful affair and, like a boil, you couldn't see it any more.

He showed Leroy his first rough draft.

'I can see what you're getting at, Alan. Real life is very different from books and TV thrillers. The thing that bothers me, though, is whether crime is hereditary. Ellery told me last week my Dad won't be coming back for a while. He's doing three years for fraud in Jamaica. I just wonder whether I'll be all right. Know what I mean?'

'I take after my mother,' Alan replied defensively. He'd had the notion, of course, but had quickly dismissed it from his mind.

'There's a quote from Shakespeare's *Henry V* that I find comforting.'

'Oh, not him again,' Alan moaned.

'He's the greatest, man . . . just you believe me. He's

got lots to tell us. You and I have lots of disadvantages. We don't have the best of health; we don't have money and neither of us is going to be a university professor. When you've finished your essay put this at the bottom of it.' He wrote the quote on the back of an envelope.

Gary surprised the Hogans a week later. He arrived at the flat full of himself. He'd won two tickets in the Andertons Garage Promotions Draw for a trip to Paris from the new Stolport. He'd wangled two more from undisclosed sources and proposed to take them all for a weekend in Paris. Marcia was too dumbfounded to refuse. They had a wonderful time and Marcia, although she cried a lot, got through the weekend without taking a single tablet.

Miss Twist took the essays home to mark them. She smiled knowingly when she came to the end of Alan's piece. She could recognise Leroy's quotes by now, and she knew for certain that Alan had never read, and never would read, Shakespeare's *Henry V*. The quote read:

> 'The strawberry grows underneath the nettle
> And wholesome berries thrive and ripen best
> Neighboured by fruit of baser quality'

After writing a few critical and helpful comments she added, 'A sound and perceptive piece, especially for such a green strawberry.'